RELEASE
YOUR UNSTOPPABLE
POWER
the journey continues...

KIERAN REVELL
FOREWORD BY BILL BARTMANN

Rationale for Cover

THE EXTRAORDINARY POWER OF HUMANITY

The lighthouse has an indomitable presence. It stands proud and strong, illuminating a pathway through the edge of darkness and uncertainty. It signifies the strength, courage and resilience of the human spirit.

The light which shines forth, typifies the innate power of humanity to selflessly assist others on their journeys through those periods of gloom and indecision.

The ocean is the life and strength of opportunity. It carries us towards success and prosperity in a joyful and optimistic future; that brilliant tapestry, represented by the sunrise on the horizon.

The picture stands as a reminder to keep working with enthusiasm and passion towards the realization of your life's purpose. In so doing, you have the capacity to create something extraordinary in your own life and in the lives of others.

TESTIMONIALS

This book gives you power, purpose and direction to overcome any obstacle and achieve any goal you can set for yourself

BRIAN TRACY
Author, *The Power of Self-Confidence*

Kieran continues the theme of personal and professional enrichment in this very powerful book.

Like his first, (*The Unstoppable Power Within*) this too is written in a very easy to understand style. The content is very powerful, designed specifically to help anyone create exactly the life desired - irrespective of means or circumstances.

DR. JOE RUBINO
Creator highselfesteemkids.com
lifeoptimizationcoaching.com

Kieran Revell has once again created a truly extraordinary book, which has the power to change our lives for the better, if we but use the principles he shares.

Kieran is not only a fantastic author but also a great storyteller who uses that talent to bring universal truths to the reader in simple but elegant words. Just open the book and start reading. You'll be happy you did.

JOHN HARRICHARAN
Award-winning, bestselling author

In his newest book, *Release Your Unstoppable Power*, Kieran Revell presents us with yet another powerful guide to learning to embrace success.

Follow the plan which Kieran has so succinctly laid out and realize the power you have to be the very best possible you. Step into your power and 'unleash' your genius today.

JIM DONOVAN
Author, *What Are You Waiting For? It's Your Life*

We all began this journey in Kieran's first book, and now we get the chance to finish our journey within. This book will help us to never underestimate the power we have inside.

JIM STOVALL

Author, *The Ultimate Gift*

Stop procrastinating and act. Shine a bright light on your future. There are absolutely no excuses for failure.

Read this wonderful work and begin the process of permanent, positive change in your life.

DENIS WAITLEY

Author, *The New Winner's Edge*

Kieran has once again delivered an amazing blueprint for success. Like his first publication, *The Unstoppable Power Within*, Kieran has eloquently provided each and every one of us with a clear and unambiguous pathway to a prosperous future.

Kieran's personal stories are powerful and moving. His quotations are literally life changing, and as with his first book, I believe *Unleash Your Unstoppable Power* will also be used as a reference book in the future.

TERRY HAWKINS (CSP)

MD and Founder—People In Progress Global

Professional Speaker and Educator

Author, *Why Wait to be Great? It's Either Now & Too Late* and

Flipman® Rules (Children's Series)

Not only is this book a terrific source of encouragement, it's also a blueprint you can use to create a bold, beautiful and brilliant life.

Make no mistake—it will require effort on your part, but if you can apply what you learn here you will release the power inside you in a magnificent way.

JOSH HINDS

Founder of GetMotivation.com

Author, *It's Your Life, Live Big*

Release Your Unstoppable Power is Kieran's second extraordinary book. It continues the journey of self-fulfillment he began in his first exceptional publication, *The Unstoppable Power Within*. This second gem is as amazing as the first.

Every chapter presents the reader with a lesson in life. Together they make up a very powerful program for personal and professional enrichment.

I have known Kieran for many years and understand his drive and purpose. He is truly a man on a mission: To improve the world, one person; one mind; one attitude at a time.

If you are serious about creating the ideal life then today is the time to move forward and begin your remarkable journey of discovery.

Walk out from the shadows and take the first step: Buy this exceptional book and use it as your launching pad.

GLENN B. BOURKE (M. Ed)
Professor of Communication
Mentor and Motivational Speaker

This book is full of great wisdom and will have a lasting effect on your commitments, choices and dreams!

Harness your personal forces and chart your own course to success – Kieran Revell shows you how in this remarkable book. Anyone committed to his or her own development will appreciate the revelations found here!

Kieran has adroitly shown how developing the right mindset and the right plan can help you transcend heretofore-insurmountable obstacles – you will be amazed at the results!

Marshall Goldsmith
Author, the *New York Times* and global bestseller
What Got You Here Won't Get You There

In this book, Kieran delivers a powerful framework through which we can more easily create a very rich and powerful future. *Release Your Unstoppable Power* establishes itself as a positive and driven program for those who are serious about realizing their dream of prosperity.

Read this superb work and begin the transformation process required to go from your Current Reality to your Preferred Reality... You'll be glad you did.

JERRY 'DRHINO' CLARK
Chief Empowerment Officer
Author, *The Art of Transformation*
ClubRhino.com

Kieran is an absolute genius with words. His encapsulated wisdom in the form of original inspirational quotes alone, is worth your investment in this book.

His recipe for success will resonate with the very core of your being. Continue your journey with him to uncover your imaginable possibilities. Embrace self-belief and your future becomes unlimited.

DR.YKK (YEW KAM KEONG, PH.D)
Business Innovation Speaker and Bestselling Author

Kieran Revell's great new book *Release Your Unstoppable Power*, delivers a powerful framework within which we can so easily create a much more enriched life.

This is a defining book, designed specifically to help anyone – an individual, group or organization - irrespective of means or circumstances, to create exactly the life desired.

EVA GREGORY
Author, *The Feel Good Guide to Prosperity*

Kieran's kindness and caring come through all that he does, like a breath of spring air, that elevates all of those he touches.

All of us can learn, grow and be reminded of the good and beautiful things through his work.

RIDGELY GOLDSBOROUGH
The WHY Guy

In this wonderful book *Release Your Unstoppable Power*, Kieran has woven an extraordinary story of hope and faith, with beautiful words and phrases. These are timeless principles that I have applied in my life.

His personal quotes stand alone and are astonishing. Through the chapters, they assist in weaving a magnificent fabric upon which we can safely and securely build an extraordinary future.

Every aspect of this book is an integral component of a true life-enriching plan. It offers a very comprehensive, step by step blueprint for living the most astonishing life possible.

I recommend *Release Your Unstoppable Power* to everyone seeking to improve life, encourage passion and inspiration and promote success and prosperity.

Dame DC CORDOVA
CEO, Excellerated Business Schools for Entrepreneurs/Money & You
http://www.DCCordova.com

If you want to be empowered and live the most incredible life possible, begin your inspired journey right now. Adopt the principles as Kieran has outlined in this second amazing book and watch your life transform before your eyes.

Release Your Unstoppable Power outlines everything you need to begin instigating the changes necessary to live the life you've only ever visited in your dreams.

This wonderful publication continues the theme of personal and professional enrichment which Kieran set out so succinctly in his first life-enriching book (*The Unstoppable Power Within*).

What are you waiting for? Start the process of success and prosperity today. Believe in yourself, take the necessary action and watch as your amazing future begins to unfold.

NATALIE LEDWELL
Bestselling author and co-founder of Mind Movies

In this wonderful book, *Release Your Unstoppable Power*, Kieran Revell provides you with a blueprint for success. Regardless of where you are in life, you will be moved to take the necessary steps to create the life you truly desire.

BOB PROCTOR
Bestselling author of *You Were Born Rich*

Not all self-help books live up to their promises, but *Release Your Unstoppable Power* does. Kieran does an excellent job of explaining how to visualize and set goals in the most clear-cut way. He takes you from the beginning of the goal realization process all the way to the end.

Probably the best part about this book is the "Lessons Learned" recap at the end of each chapter, where he goes over everything just covered so that readers don't lose track.

I strongly recommend this empowering work to anyone regardless of where they are in life. The transformation will be so worth it.

CHRISTIAN MICKELSEN
CEO, Future Force, Inc.
www.CoachesWithClients.com

RELEASE

YOUR UNSTOPPABLE

POWER

the journey continues...

KIERAN REVELL

Sound Wisdom
P.O. Box 310
Shippensburg, PA 17257-0310

For more information on foreign distribution, call 717-530-2122.

Reach us on the Internet: www.soundwisdom.com.

ISBN 13 TP: 978-0-7684-0883-6
ISBN 13 Ebook: 978-0-7684-0884-3

For Worldwide Distribution, Printed in the U.S.A.
1 2 3 4 5 6 7 8 / 19 18 17 16 15

When you love and respect yourself without reservation, it's enough to quietly hold it firmly in your heart. Those emotions will illuminate the journey into the future. Others will gladly follow your shining light.

—KIERAN REVELL, 1996

DEDICATION

This book is dedicated with heartfelt love and affection to:

My beautiful Suzanne—the love of my life.
You bring sunshine into every aspect of my world.
My wonderful son Kayle,
The most creative person I know.
I truly love you both beyond words.

ACKNOWLEDGMENTS

The consciousness of just one positive and compassionate
soul has the capacity to change the world. Imagine what a
group of optimistic, focused, and passionate people can do.

Life has a way of offering gifts that might at first appear to be wrapped in a challenge or obstacle. When I face mine, it's heartwarming to know I have wonderful people in my life who are happy to stand by me through the good and not so good times.

I remain so grateful to my beautiful wife Suzanne who has the biggest and warmest heart on the planet. Nothing is ever too much trouble. Her common sense approach to everyday life keeps my head just a short distance from the clouds. We have endured some dark moments and celebrated so many more magic times together.

My son Kayle is a wonderful young man who also has a big heart. He has an awesome intellect and an unsurpassed creative flair. He makes me smile every day as he goes from strength to strength with his imagination and ingenuity.

Suzanne and Kayle are the two key links in my gold chain of life. I'm eternally grateful for their ongoing love, support, and encouragement.

Thank you to Dr. YKK for his input to the Rationale for Cover. He has a unique way of seeing the big picture and quickly getting to the core of any issue.

Thanks to Jim (Gymbeaux) Brown for his valuable time and assistance. His eye for detail has helped me greatly.

Last but not least, a *huge* thank you to the amazing team at Sound Wisdom Publishing. I am forever grateful for your continued support of me as an author, speaker, and consultant. I am exceedingly proud to walk beside you.

David Wildasin, John Martin, Tammy Fitzgerald, and Eileen Rockwell are integral members of that team. Thank you for your enthusiasm, encouragement, and extraordinary attention to detail.

A big thank you to all my loyal readers, clients, and supporters. You are also my friends. Enjoy the journey ahead as, together, we grasp new opportunities and embrace brand new horizons.

Every day I have unprecedented opportunities to meet with some amazing people across all walks of life. I have countless moments of joy with memories I can cherish forever.

Imagine the possibilities....

With an unwavering self-belief and the courage to pursue our dreams, we become much stronger with the passion, power, and determination to face and overcome even great obstacles—the inevitable sunshine after struggle.

CONTENTS

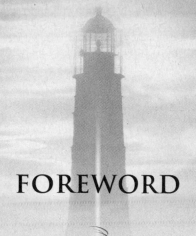

FOREWORD

Having come from a very limiting background, I understand the value of a dream. I also understand the necessity for a plan of action and the vision, determination, and passion to fire it. Your dream will always be relegated to the confines of your subconscious mind if you do nothing about it. Through this powerful book, the reader has at last been given an easy-to-follow strategy to make those dreams a reality and realize true success and prosperity in life.

In this decisive work, Kieran lays bare the myth of simple attraction and outlines a very precise step-by-step guide for the individual who has a desire to create the ideal life. Through this very well constructed program, you at last have a road map to success, embodied with great color, depth, and enormous clarity. The various chapters are designed to take you on a journey of discovery of the many aspects of your life and the incredibly exciting journey on which you are about to embark.

It is never enough to simply rely on good luck to deliver the existence you desire. You can never wish for a better life and hope it will manifest. It will simply not occur. If you are tired of your current circumstances—living each day from hand to mouth and struggling to realize any level of affluence—and you wish for success and prosperity in all aspects of your life, you need to read this book to understand what is necessary to get you to that defining moment.

In *The Unstoppable Power Within*, I believe Kieran has written a true blueprint for a better life. This compelling book outlines an easy-to-follow approach to creating a prosperous and abundant life. It has the capacity to take you from where you are right now to an incredible destination. Up until this very moment you might not have even dared dream of arriving at that amazing place.

This is a powerful and extremely well written book. It highlights the fundamental steps necessary to deliver you the ideal life. If you are sick of dreaming and hoping and you really want a better existence for yourself, your family, and your company, get this book today, read it, and put the principles into practice right now.

Your future will unfold regardless of what you do. Therefore, there is no better time than here and now to begin laying the foundation for the life you truly deserve. No matter who you are or what negative experiences you've had up until this moment, it is never too late to embrace success and prosperity in your world.

I recommend this empowering work to any individual or organization looking to greatly improve conditions and begin to see real and tangible results in all aspects of their daily lives.

BILL BARTMANN
Billionaire Business Coach
www.billbartmann.com

INTRODUCTION

You will only achieve and appreciate incredible success when it is accomplished without prejudice, dishonesty, hate, fear, or despair. They are true obstacles that will forever obstruct your view of the future and limit the power and reach of your accomplishments.

Eleanor Roosevelt, wife of the 32nd President of the United States (Franklin Delano Roosevelt) put it so eloquently when she said, *"The future belongs to those who believe in the beauty of their dreams!"*[1] Welcome to the second book of life altering information. Here we continue to delve into the power of the human spirit. Together, let's continue the journey to building a spectacular future.

Each of us has an amazing power residing deep within. It's a well of immeasurable value which forms the very essence of who we are as humans. Irrespective of what our circumstances might be, we have the capacity to be happy, healthy, and successful. Once we learn to release that power, the future becomes so much brighter and more powerful.

The information contained in the following chapters shows us how to tap into that immeasurable power. It presents a valuable blueprint for a successful future. We touch on the very relevant topics of *creative visualization, self-esteem building, change, attitude*, and many others fundamental to personal and professional development.

Like countless other people on this earth, I too have struggled to find my way in the darkness. There have been some periods of great gloom which threatened to overshadow me. Those times, however, are thankfully eclipsed by the many more instances of sheer joy which continue to fill my world.

> Each of us fosters the voice of strength, calm, and reason inside. It speaks to us, according to our needs: The happy voice, the thin voice, the self-respect, wealth, success, health, and contentment voice. Learn to listen and respond without doubt or recrimination.

I know what it's like to struggle, to experience total darkness and uncertainty, facing those seemingly insurmountable obstacles alone and feeling helpless in the face of almost total gloom and despair. Sometimes it can appear hopeless as we struggle to find a glimmer of hope in the wilderness.

I also know how your life can change when opportunities come knocking and you're in the right place at the right time, with the right frame of mind to embrace them. It becomes one of the greatest feelings in life. Irrespective of means or circumstance, it can happen to each and every one of us at any time.

Every moment of every day has an effect on our life because each one is filled with thoughts, words, actions, feelings, and emotions. They leave an imprint on us and on those with whom we interact. Together, they help to forge the future. When we act with respect, trust, gratitude, pride, passion, drive, and commitment we put ourselves in a far better position to recognize opportunities as they arise and subsequently capitalize on them.

> Irrespective of the amount of pressure you find yourself under, remain positive and upbeat and always focus on the end prize. Sooner or later you'll emerge as a priceless diamond.

Success and prosperity don't happen by coincidence. They are not accidents or incidents that somehow fall at our feet. I know of very few people who dream of a better life and, when they wake, find awesome wealth and personal prosperity waiting anxiously in the closet. I'm afraid that only happens in films. Approach the topic diligently and passionately. Understand you will be in for the long haul and continue to treat the whole journey with professionalism.

Your life is a business enterprise. It's your own economy requiring a solid investment of time, energy, emotion, absolute belief, determination, and money. It takes an unremitting effort to continue on this empowered journey. Know where you're going, remain focused and determined, and divest yourself of all the doubts and fears holding you back.

Society is brimming with exceptional people with a unique understanding of how the world works and the nature of the universal laws governing success and abundance. These inspired individuals remain sanguine as they constantly forge a path toward their goals, irrespective of the obstacles faced.

They are just like you and me. They have dreams and goals, driven by their determination. They remain confident that their focus, vision, and solid plan of action will see them achieve all they desire, while the pitfalls they encounter are merely steps along the way to realizing (and sometimes realigning) their goals.

These driven individuals display a profound courage and commitment in the face of struggle and refuse to allow obstacles to stand in the way of their pursuit of success and prosperity. They are abundantly clear about who they are, what they want in their lives, and how to go about achieving those desires.

Triumph is born not simply from great success, but also temporary failure from which lessons are invariably learned.

The past *does not* equal the future, and though it can and generally does have some impact on our lives, we should not allow what has occurred to adversely affect the direction we're traveling *now*. Ensure the choices you make are positively driven, based on your true desires, passions, and dreams. Put that plan into action and fuel it in the direction you want to go.

The clouds will part and the sun shine even more brightly on and in your life as you realize the power you have to change your situation. A better and more abundant life is at your fingertips...waiting.

Hitch your wagon to your plan of action; release negativity and drive forward with enthusiasm and determination. Success through opportunity is there to be embraced and provide untapped optimism on your magnificent journey. It's often the impact of adversity that enables us to view our life with greater clarity. It allows us to surge forward with a new and driven mentality. We release ourselves from pessimism as we set our sights on the horizon ahead.

Think clearly and remain focused on your goals and dreams at all times. Have the resolve to look inside for inspiration. Foster that belief in your own wonderful inner power, and don't allow adverse factors (including pessimistic thoughts from yourself and others) to impede your perception.

It's not the gravitational pull of suffering that should drive you; rather, the ever present (though often repressed) knowledge that you are incredible and capable of so much more in your life.

Success is possible in the lives of each of us, no matter our individual circumstances. We must first believe we deserve it; then plan, prepare, and fully expect it, without doubt.

There are those who constantly think of new and innovative ideas but don't actually convert them into reality (they remain simply dreams), while others begin and successfully complete project after project (converting dreams into reality).

Even within our own circles, many start but fail to complete projects while others seem to sign off on them one after another. There are those who try very hard but can't seem to finish in first place, when others constantly stand triumphantly at the podium for whatever activity they undertake.

It can happen in the confines of the home; in the office, the supermarket, the gym, or on the sporting field; perhaps in the street, the car, your garden, or at the home of friends. None of us knows where or when problems will strike or in what manner or intensity. It depends on various factors—the quality of your life; the actions (and inactions) you take; the company you keep; the degree of interaction with others and the environment; your state of mind; belief in your journey and how you think you figure in the big scheme of things; your understanding of your innate abilities and the degree of self-belief and feelings of self-worth you cultivate. The world is a big place, true enough, but it need not be daunting.

Take from this work what you need to move forward with confidence. Use the content to build your life, fortify your actions, and increase your confidence. Each of us has an exceptional destiny; we need to embrace it fully with courage and determination. We can have everything we need to realize it provided we plan, organize, and fully expect it to happen.

We are all worthy of great things and should never allow the negativity that infiltrates our lives from time to time to derail us from our purpose.

Enjoy your journey and never be afraid of setbacks. Use them as stepping stones to strengthen your resolve. You are on the path to fulfillment; you need only believe that to be so above all else and take the steps necessary to bring success into your life. Lay out the red carpet and invite prosperity to enter.

Imagine the possibilities...

Problems are like potholes in the road—often unavoidable. However, having stepped in one, you can choose to step out and move on, or you can decide to stay where you are and wallow in self-pity. The future will unfold regardless. —KIERAN

NOTE

1   Eleanor Roosevelt, qtd. in Leonard C. Schlup and Donald W. Whisenhunt, *It Seems to Me: Selected Letters of Eleanor Roosevelt* (Lexington, KY: University Press of Kentucky, 2001), 2.

Chapter 1

THE IMPORTANCE OF GOAL-SETTING

A goal must be more than a simple notion, wish, or dream of something better. Once you see it in all its warmth and color and empower it with a strong and committed plan of action, you will truly believe in your capacity to succeed.

Goal-setting is intrinsically about empowerment and striving for achievement. It is stimulated by constant and ongoing creative thinking and motivation. This is built on a specific foundation and driven by an intense desire or pressing need for improvement. Very often it becomes the journey to uncover and embrace your purpose.

In my early years, goal-setting was something I never thought a great deal about. The struggle with my speech stammer almost consumed me as I grappled with the bullying and constant environment of negativity. I really couldn't see much past the darkness that surrounded me. At that stage in my life, there weren't too many bright lights (see About Kieran Revell p. 249).

However, as I emerged from the fog and started building my life, I gained a much greater understanding of the value of setting goals. The process gave me something positive to work toward. It began to grow in importance because as I set goals and began achieving them, my confidence grew. My thinking became more positive and much clearer. Setting and achieving became easier to do.

Irrespective of who we are, we all have goals of varying degrees. Many are potentially life-changing, while others are less important, day-to-day commitments. I certainly have them. I know you do too.

For many years I was constantly fascinated by homelessness. I just couldn't understand how or why it occurred, especially in developed countries. It seemed to be a taboo topic which people avoided. It did intrigue me.

As years passed, I realized I needed to better understand people. It was then I made up my mind to set myself the real challenge. I wanted to add value to the world. To do that, I had to understand the residents. I knew how people of reasonable affluence lived. I counted my blessings every day because my parents instilled in me great values. I was born into a middle class home and never wanted for anything: However, I knew very little about the poorer people of the world— the disenfranchised and forgotten. It became my focus.

I decided I would somehow spend time with homeless people to better understand their plight. I didn't know when or how, though I did know the opportunity would present itself when the time was right.

> Once you understand the power of creative visualization to manifest positive occurrences and opportunities in your life, you'll know beyond question that you've taken the crucial steps toward the wonderfully inspiring phenomenon of attraction. Prepare to be amazed.

On the spur of the moment, I made the decision to achieve that goal in 1997. Without telling anyone in my life what I intended (apart from telling a few selected people I was going away for a week and would probably not be contactable), I filled a small backpack with some necessities; I put on some old, worn clothes and with $150 in my pocket (for food and other contingencies) set out for the streets of Sydney. I really didn't know what to expect, but I knew in my heart it was the right thing to do.

During that enlightening time I got to know many people, some of whom had been otherwise successful business professionals. I slept in the open; I bought take away food; I spent time watching, talking, and taking notes. It was one of the most empowering periods of my life. It was also one of the most frightening times.

I came away with a brand new perspective on life. I realized how blessed I am and decided to use the experience to assist others. I was able to understand and appreciate the true value of goal-setting.

As an aside, when I picked up my belongings and decided to return home, I gave the money I had collected during that time ($112.17) to a homeless man named "Tony." He thought I was crazy!

The primary objective in goal-setting is to pinpoint the end result through your thought processes and set about achieving your desires. Setting goals indicates a drive to have in our lives the things that empower us and makes us feel good about ourselves. It's also about our wish to provide wonderful things for our families to make life easier, more comfortable, and fulfilling.

Many people labor in a job they detest, earning a wage they believe does not represent their true worth. They live in a house they don't like and drive an old clunker of a car. They often feel trapped—as if shackled by a ball and chain—wandering about aimlessly in ever-decreasing circles.

The negativity in the lives of these people ultimately affects all aspects of their being. It contributes to a bad attitude. It also adversely impacts relationships. This need not be the case once they understand the power they have to create an extraordinary future through functional goal-setting (and a much more positive attitude).

Wherever possible and in spite of what challenges we face, it's important to do what we love and love what we do. It was the great science fiction, horror, and fantasy author Ray Bradbury who so succinctly said, *"Love what you do and do what you love. Don't listen to anyone else who tells you not to do it. You do what you want, what you love. Imagination should be the center of your life."*[1]

There will often be aspects of your job, your home, the car you drive, or the neighborhood where you live that have positive elements attached. Find out what they are and link with them. This is the first step to making your life brighter until you can move or make significant adjustments.

There's no doubt goal-setting is a powerful tool in all aspects of your life. It remains a fundamental part of your success strategy. There's no magic involved, and no matter how difficult and out of control your life can at times seem, you are in charge of your own destiny. You have at your fingertips the ability to design the life you want, irrespective of where you are at a particular moment and the challenges you might face on your journey. You must understand the need to put in place some solid and positive structure to begin the process of realizing your goals.

> This is the list of reasons you should adopt when considering the many reasons for delaying the pursuit of your goals: There are none.

A trigger for your imagination will commence the process of functional goal-setting. You have to fuel your desire by committing to paper exactly what it is you want. According to studies, about 3 percent of people actually go through this very important process of recording their goals.[2] It begs the question, *"If goals are so important, why don't people give more time to clearly setting them?"*

In my experience, people think it's a waste of time writing down their goals when they could be out doing something concrete about realizing them. If they only knew that writing them is the first and most important step in the realization process.

Write your goals in your diary or journal (see Chapter 5: "Your Mandatory Diary/Journal") and constantly revise them according to changing circumstances. Whether they're short term (immediate to one year), medium (one to five years), or long term (five-plus years), when you commit them to paper you immediately become more focused and your goals become clearer.

For long-term goals, write down where you intend to be in 20 years or more—where you're living, the job you have and kind of lifestyle you're enjoying: the assets and financial base you accumulate. Write those goals very explicitly in your diary/journal and on your Creation Board (see Chapter 4: "Your Indispensable Creation Board") and understand the various processes involved in attaining them.

Use them as guides to develop in your mind—a clear description of exactly where it is you want to be and what you want in your life. Take yourself there and experience the results; realize them and understand how it feels to experience them in all their glory. Feel, smell, see, taste, and hold them in your hands and your mind. Put that ball into play immediately.

> Greatness is not measured in terms of achievement, but rather in the self-belief and courage to strive for (perceived unobtainable) goals. Achievement will surely come.

When you come back to the present, hold the images in your mind and use them as a platform to launch your plan for a more remarkable future. Use this very important tool as often as possible so your goals become a concrete part of your psyche. They must become an everyday component of your thinking, breathing, and living.

> Phenomenal success is within your grasp. It is truly tangible and attainable. Create it by building on your dreams and setting goals. Believe in them with every fiber of your being, and give them the passion and effort required. The universe will respond.

Be precise in what you want in relation to your goal-setting. It's not enough to simply think, "I'd love a lot of money in the bank and a great car." It has no foundation or thrust. Develop a strong base with some real inspiration and begin establishing your goals. Be clear, concise, and colorful. Write them in your journal and put them on your Creation Board. Partner them with complimenting photographs. This could be done in the following way:

- I'm looking and feeling better every day, because I exercise regularly and eat well.

- Every day I'm becoming more inspired and successful, because I believe in myself and have faith in my ability to be victorious.

- I'm have a wonderful home life, because I love my family and friends and am supported by them.

- I'm building a strong and abundant business through hard work, planning, and determination.

- Every day is bringing me good health, happiness, love, and prosperity.

In addition to the above information, you'll find some very supportive steps to achieving success in your New Year Resolutions (see Chapter 2: "New Year Resolutions"). These can also be used in setting and achieving your specific goals at any time of the year.

The race you run in your life differs from that of any other person. Your goals are different, and therefore, your preparation should be unique to you.

Don't compare yourself to others irrespective of how you may be feeling at any given time. Jealousy, envy, and frustration are negative emotions to be avoided at all costs. Your best yardstick of success is yourself. Do things today a little better, longer, and more passionately than you did yesterday. Achieving success is never about winning or losing—it isn't a race—it's about making improvements to your life, whatever you consider those changes to be. The degree of modification is up to you, depending upon where you want to go in your life and what you wish to be, do, and experience.

Setting goals is one of the first steps on the ladder to achievement. They are the light at the end of the tunnel toward which you direct your energy, focus, and determination.

The bigger the dream, the bigger the reality—that's an unambiguous and undisputed truth. The lives of those who strive for and achieve the absolute best remain testimony to the very core of that adage. Constantly reach for the stars—they are well and truly within your grasp. Always reward yourself for even the smallest successes. Self-recognition is a concrete support mechanism for elevating self-worth. It boosts your confidence and makes you generally feel good about your actions.

Don't ever feel lucky or, conversely, guilty for achievement. Always fill your heart and mind with gratitude for even the smallest blessings. Similarly, if you fall short of your goal, you should understand that everything occurs for a specific purpose. Give yourself a small penalty (take something away) as an indication that you are truly focused on the prize and you know you can do better. *All actions have consequences.* Stick by this rule; it will give your life greater balance for the maintenance and support of your journey. Refrain from rebuking yourself or feeling as if you're letting yourself down. This is counter-productive and can derail you from your true purpose (see Chapter 2: "New Year Resolutions").

Dream big dreams, because attached to them are big goals and even bigger rewards.

Many historical achievements have been preceded by periods of difficulty and sacrifice. Similarly, many of your days will be filled with challenge; however, hard work and persistence are always rewarded. When you feel happy and content with the outcome of your effort and dedication—where your reality exceeds your dream—reward yourself with a gift because you set worthwhile goals and systematically achieved them.

Continue to focus on the present and ensure what you're doing now is designed to add value to the final outcome. Don't behave in a manner contrary to your morality or your goals. Make your present totally congruent with your clear and impassioned vision of the future. Refrain from putting value on negative words, thoughts, and actions that have impacted you in the past. Through their very nature, they have the capacity to impact you in the future—a place, a state of mind, and a wonderful existence that depends upon how you perform today.

> No matter the size of your dreams, once you can pinpoint an exact moment in your world when you made the decision to change for the better, you will begin to give them real life and power.

Take control of your life now and direct it where you want it to go. If you don't, it can so easily fall in a heap and become a dark and miserable place. Alternatively, with effort, focus, and determination it can become a utopia. Lead by example—with courage, passion, vision, and determination. Strength comes from within and affects those around you in a very real sense. With this positive mindset, you inadvertently assist those other people to do the same. They find power in your life-affirming action that in turn fuels your forward momentum.

In focusing on success, you should also clearly envisage the future; they are linked. Fire your imagination with your goals and dreams. They are powerful tools to accelerate abundance in your life. Picture everything in your future as a vivid and full color image through the window of opportunity—literally. Daydream about how you *know* things will turn out, whether it's the great new job, car, the house, holiday, or relationship. See yourself in the position *now*, with color and clarity. Feel the excitement, enthusiasm, and exhilaration resulting from living the perfect life—the one you create yourself.

> When you realize the benefit of applying drive, focus, and determination to your dreams and goals, you'll be amazed at just how far your energy and passion can take you.

When you can learn to like and respect who you are and welcome the person you see yourself becoming, you gain a much deeper understanding of the power you have to accomplish any and all goals you set for your future. If you don't like something about yourself or your life and believe it's holding you back from achieving everything you want, set about instigating programs and policies for change. They will assist you to evolve into that person who has the ability and capacity to recognize and capitalize upon opportunities as they present themselves in your life. Don't hesitate or drag your feet; do it now and do it with passion and purpose.

Understand that your dreams, visions, and determination will give you the courage and strength to evolve into an even more wonderful and empowered human being. You must first believe it.

Like and respect who you are now. Allow yourself to evolve into that equally special person who is becoming even more magnificent, courageous, powerful, determined, passionate, and successful. Remain upbeat and enthusiastic about the reality you are creating through your dreams and visions.

Always envisage the best possible outcomes for yourself in everything you undertake and in all areas of your magnificent life. Hold in your mind a picture of yourself as a strong, passionate, and successful person striding confidently through a wonderful and colorful life. Continue your dreams as powerful tools for creating the most amazing life possible through seeing yourself as you would love to be. Once you allow yourself that freedom, your amazing journey has really commenced.

Great strides towards even greater goals are made by leaders, not followers.

As you begin to achieve your goals, systematically set more, you're moving methodically toward the next exciting chapter of your life. Success will appear at your door in different forms, and therefore it's important you don't allow yourself to become disillusioned with any setbacks. Success often arrives slower than anticipated. It can also come in the form of a challenge or obstacle.

Learn patience as your first rule—one of life's great virtues. It will allow you to recognize success as it ventures into and through your life and more capably embrace opportunities as you see them.

> The more belief you have in your life, the more you will have to believe in.

Ensure you constantly evaluate your goals and, where necessary, update them to reflect the direction you're traveling in your life at any given moment, your changing desires, and the opportunities presented. Building on your goals indicates your intention to remain results-driven and focused. It also enables you to remain on track as you move forward with persistence and determination.

Never seek to go through your life in a hurry. You will miss so much. Life is a series of successes where prosperity will come to you in many forms and at varying times, provided you lay the solid foundation and open your mind and your heart. Success will continue to rise up and meet you along life's journey when you remain focused on your goals and dreams and continue working diligently to achieve them. A positive attitude will allow you to enjoy the voyage of discovery and continue to learn lessons along the way.

> Failure is not one phenomenon occurring spontaneously in your life. It's the combination of a number of contributing factors you don't recognize and take steps to avoid.

Patience is not easy to learn and adopt. Take your time to appreciate and understand your journey. Never be in a hurry to get "there," wherever that mystical place might be. Set your goal, lay out your plan, color your dreams and visions, and be persistent. Above all, be patient.

As you begin to recognize the little signs of achievement along the way—no matter how seemingly insignificant these might appear—you'll begin to feel empowered and more confident as each day passes and every step is fulfilled. Learn to have gratitude for these little moments of empowerment and use them as stepping stones to that wonderfully abundant future.

Congratulate yourself when you achieve the successes and feel proud as they are taking you closer to your future. Every small success is a milestone and a goal in itself, so savor the moment and ensure you write the achievements in your diary/journal (see Chapter 5: "Your Mandatory Diary/Journal").

> If you don't allow yourself to have big dreams, you'll never have the capacity to accept big successes in your life.

Even when you feel deflated and your back is against the wall, summon the strength and courage to fill your heart and your head with reasons why you can and should continue in spite of opposition. When you feel yourself falling off the wagon or detouring from your path, simply go back to the reasons why you started the quest in the first place.

Continue to dream of the goals you've set yourself to achieve that wonderful life and reach the incredible destination you know without doubt awaits you. Don't stop believing in your life and your destiny. Continue to empower yourself and never allow negativity to deter you and push you from your path.

Have courage and always focus on the prize. Do everything in your power to overcome those obstacles that might sometimes obscure your view of the path ahead. See them as they really are—guideposts to show you the way ahead.

Refrain from the lure of mediocrity through complacency and inaction. Nurture that faith in yourself, your goals, and the skills and creativity you possess to achieve them.

You will overcome any fear you have of goal-setting if you simply make the decision to take action now. The only real fear you have is fear itself. See past it, and take whatever life-enriching steps are necessary to succeed. All things are possible if you only believe.

NOTES

1. *A Conversation with Ray Bradbury*, dir. Lawrence Bridges, feat. Ray Bradbury, September 11, 2008, https://www.youtube.com/watch?v=EzD0YtbViCs#t=444.

2. Kevin Eikenberry, "Seven Reasons People Don't Set Goals," Inside Indiana Business, accessed February 15, 2015, http://www.insideindianabusiness.com/contributors.asp?id=877.

Whenever I permit others to impact negatively on my life, I will be unable to welcome abundance and success in all its forms.

LESSONS LEARNED

1. Goal-setting is an incredibly powerful tool for achievement.

2. You're always in control of your own destiny.

3. Avoid comparing yourself and your life with another.

4. Achievements will always serve to silence your detractors.

5. Courage and strength come from dreams, goals, and determination.

6. Like and respect yourself now for who you are and what you have achieved thus far.

7. Never wish for a speedy life. Enjoy the journey to fulfillment.

8. Be grateful for all moments of empowerment on your journey.

9. Always think of reasons why you can/should do certain things—then do them.

10. Never stop believing in yourself and your destiny.

11. Don't allow darkness and negativity to invade your life. Fill your existence with sunshine.

12. All things in life are truly possible. You have only to work hard and believe.

13. Have courage and always focus on the prize.

14. Never succumb to the darkness of mediocrity through complacency and inaction.

Chapter 2

NEW YEAR RESOLUTIONS

Every day in every conceivable way, my life is
becoming a more worthwhile and fulfilled place.

I have always believed in New Year resolutions. At the very least, I always
seemed to make them and, more often than not, I realize many of them—losing weight, getting fit, going to certain places for holidays, getting out and
meeting people, and generally making positive changes to my life.

In June of 2013, after sending the manuscript for my first book, *The
Unstoppable Power Within,* to countless publishing houses and receiving negative responses (and often no response at all), I made up my mind to have my
book accepted by a mainstream publishing house, no matter how long it took.

I wasn't sure how or when but I knew it would happen. In my mind's eye I
began to *see* the book in print and experience the feelings of elation at actually
having a mainstream publication. It was the key to open the door for me to do
what I consider to be *my purpose.*

I began to picture all the good I could do when I gained an international
profile and built a strong platform. I have so many projects to be greatly
assisted through gaining some recognition. Doors to influential people open,
allowing them to see what I have to offer and the amount of good I can do

with the material I have developed over the years. I was positive and focused. I refused to allow the setbacks to bring me down. I used them instead as fuel for my journey.

> The word "no" only becomes a constant in our lives when we accept it as the inevitable result.

After so many years people said to me, "Do you think it might be time to give it away?" "How will you feel in twenty years' time if you're still trying to open doors?" "I wish I had your persistence and determination." Those who know me understand my push. They knew I would never give up. I knew in my heart I had a wonderful product that would benefit so many people on a global scale. I refused to surrender.

I continued to send the manuscript out and even took the drastic step of submitting it to a vanity publishing house. It was also uploaded to the Internet. Throughout this protracted period, I refused to surrender my dream.

Though I found the experience practically useless, I realized it wasn't a mistake because I know there are none in life. It proved to be a very good lesson which taught me many things. Best of all, it taught me the value of commitment.

I have continued to refine the work, largely through adding new chapters and altering others. I've generally updated the material to get it to a point where I am happy with the content. I decided to do the entire initial edit myself because I was able to take an objective view of the entire manuscript.

I asked for and received dozens of endorsements for the book from the world's leading speakers and coaches. I have absolute faith in the power of the book and its capacity to change lives. I knew in my heart it was worthy of publication. I believed in myself. I believed in my dreams and goals. I certainly believe in my book.

One morning in January 2014, I was at home on the computer. I was writing furiously when the phone rang. When I answered it, I was taken aback for a moment. The voice on the other end of the phone told me he represented a mainstream publishing house in Pennsylvania. The ensuing conversation was to change my life forever.

This is my second book so I can tell you that making resolutions does work. I will continue to do it until I close my eyes for the final time.

The notion of the New Year resolution is believed to date back to about 150 BC, to the time of Janus, the mythical Roman God of Gates and Doors. It was a time which represented new beginnings. According to mythology, Janus had two faces and could look forward to the future and back on his past. Because of his position, he was placed at the head of the calendar and became the symbol of hope and resolution. The beginning of the year became a period where Romans sought forgiveness from enemies and exchanged gifts with friends, family members, and neighbors to welcome in the New Year.

Even today it signifies new beginnings. It's a time when an individual can systematically build on past gains, rectify any hiccups, and remove obstacles in a very firm resolve to move forward with optimism, courage, and passion. In many countries, the New Year is celebrated by a swim in open water as a form of cleansing and re-birth. (I'm not sure the thought of a dip in the North Sea during winter is my idea of a good time!)

The modern New Year's Day is a time when countless people make (often over-ambitious) promises to themselves. That being said, most of us put very little stock in these declarations. In fact, various studies have been conducted, and while the figures vary, in general terms it's believed that less than 40 percent of the population even bothers to make serious resolutions. Of those, less than 60 percent keep them after the first month, and that diminishes to about 45 percent for three months and even less beyond six months before lapsing into old ways as we forget those personal promises made.

> Make your new year's resolution an everyday promise. Constant, positive reinforcement ensures your commitment remains a priority.

The New Year is traditionally a time for reflection and introspection, when we think about the twelve months gone by and the period to follow. "What does the time ahead hold for me?" "Have I lived up to my expectations over the past twelve months?" "What can I do to be more successful?" "Will I get that new job or move house?" "Can I improve on my life and live a better and more fulfilled existence?" The questions are literally endless as we begin our soul searching.

This is the moment when we reflect on the time passed and wonder what the future holds for us. We ponder our achievements and briefly touch on those areas where we were less than vibrant. In the ideal world we ask ourselves if we have a clear and concise plan in place to help us move forward. It's the concrete required to build on what we already have, assisting us to move around obstacles and open the pathway ahead.

In these instances, a coach or mentor is a valuable person on whom we can call for assistance when the road seems to take us uphill. This person can provide us with objective feedback and assistance in building on those strong and empowered plans for the future.

> In addition to New Year resolutions and to constantly empower your dreams and goals, make solid promises to yourself for a better life and instigate ongoing changes to enrich and inspire your journey.

The New Year is a time to be grateful for the period now passed into history: "Thank you for all the love, happiness, harmony, and good health I continue to enjoy." "Thank you for the great holiday to Hawaii." "I'm grateful for the new jet-ski." "I had a fabulous eighteenth birthday party."

Irrespective of what negative influences might have impacted your life, there will always be high points. Be thankful for these instead of wasting time fretting over instances that were not as positive as you had hoped. It's at these times we're in low ebb and base our resolutions on the negativity in our minds and our pasts, rather than the positive aspects of our existence. At year's end, you'll realize you have so much to be thankful for and really understand the power of your dreams, goals, and plans when coupled with passion and determination.

Resolutions are generally treated as a joke and made out of superstition, with very little room for reflection on what can truly be achieved with commitment and focus. If you do take them seriously and wish to move forward with determination, you should understand it might be a struggle, and to assist, adopt some steps.

> When you lay plans with purpose and vision, very often circumstances will align.

As part of that drive to see them come to fruition, I urge my clients to adopt the following thirteen steps when setting their resolutions:

- *Make them reasonable and attainable* to stop from becoming disillusioned.

- *Write them down* in a number of effective ways—on your Creation Board; in your journal; perhaps as a screensaver on your computer or, on large pieces of paper you can stick on the doors, walls and mirrors around the house to constantly remind you.

- *Read them every day* to remain focused and on track.

- *Highlight your successes* with a red marker (or red font on the screensaver) so they stand out and can be used as reminders and anchor points during those moments you stray from your path.

- *Keep abreast of your journey* to more easily track your progress.

- *Give yourself a specific time frame for achievement.* "By my (age) birthday, I'm cigarette free and feel fantastic," or, "By June 30 and thanks to my fitness regimen and good diet, I am five kilos (eleven pounds) lighter."

- *Support your resolutions* with pictures and words to give them depth, color, and power.

- *Get the help and assistance necessary* to continue with a positive frame of mind.

- *Take one step at a time*—you won't become disheartened should you stumble.

- *Share them* with those close to you who can be a support when you fall behind.

- *Congratulate and reward yourself* when you reach a milestone. It's important you give yourself credit and reinforce your positive drive.

- *Be disciplined.* Approach your tasks with real vigor and determination. If you fall off track, take the action necessary to bring yourself back, but ensure you're not overtly "self-punishing." Refrain from resorting to any retaliatory action designed to hurt or offend. Make the penalty substantial (though never injurious or confidence destroying) so it acts as a simple reminder when you fall short of your specific goal, within the specified time frame.

- *Remain accountable.* Understand that all behavior—no matter how seemingly innocuous—has consequences. If you are determined to achieve your resolutions, it's imperative you make yourself accountable and refuse to reward laziness or inaction. As well as rewarding positive behavior, you should also deny yourself something small such as a television program, video, or treat as a reminder that perhaps you didn't work hard enough or could have done something in a different way. You might add an additional routine to your fitness workout regimen or study program for a month. You might even decide to clean the house, yard, or car!

According to Gary Keller, author and real estate expert and Chairman of Keller Williams Realty, you can assist and empower yourself to remain on track by forming a group of like-minded people. Connect with up to half a dozen friends, and each week meet or chat on the phone (or over the Internet) about your achievements and your intentions.

Talk about what you have achieved since the last meeting. Also mention your goals and what you've done to keep them real and valid in your life. It's a great way to remain accountable for your actions and a good reminder of why you are traveling the road you've chosen. In this way things are actually accomplished.

> Don't be afraid of what you might achieve. Instead, be more afraid of what you might not!

All actions and inactions should have specific personal consequences to cement them in your mind. If you congratulate yourself, you should also be empowered to remind yourself of any shortcomings that might have diverted you from your path.

Once you're aware of these and you adopt the principle of fairness, you'll put yourself that much further ahead and really understand the notion of resolutions and how powerful they can be. It can only serve to make you stronger and more committed.

You may consider setting goals throughout the year, rather than bombard yourself at New Year. This means you have more freedom and can set them along reasonable time lines. It will keep you focused and on track, where you'll not be so easily deterred by small setbacks.

> Failure is the culmination of negative actions and interactions we subconsciously accept and thus persistently repeat.

Constantly remind yourself why you've laid down your goals and make every effort to set time aside to review them at every opportunity. Make this a daily ritual and absorb the value of the pictures and emotions accompanying them. Even when you are riding a wave of success, never forget to refocus on your goals.

NOTE

1. John C. Norcross, Marci S. Mrykalo, and Matthew D. Blagys, "Auld Lang Syne: Success Predictors, Change Processes, and Self-reported Outcomes of New Year's Resolvers and Nonresolvers," *Journal of Clinical Psychology* 58, no. 4 (2002): 397–405, doi:10.1002/jclp.1151.

Your periods of leisure can become times of enormous gratification, when effort and persistence equal success.

LESSONS LEARNED

1. Take your New Year resolutions seriously.

2. There are thirteen steps to help you achieve your resolutions:

    - Make them reasonable and attainable
    - Write them down
    - Read them every day
    - Highlight your successes
    - Keep abreast of your journey
    - Give yourself a specific time frame
    - Support your resolutions with affirmative action
    - Get the help and assistance necessary
    - Take one step at a time
    - Share them
    - Congratulate and reward yourself
    - Be disciplined
    - Remain accountable

3. All actions and inactions have consequences.

4. Continue to set your resolutions, but put the steps in place.

5. Achievement should have rewards attached.

6. Don't be deterred by small setbacks.

7. Read your resolutions every day to keep them firmly in your mind.

Chapter 3

THE AMAZING POWER AND IMPACT OF CREATIVE VISUALIZATION

When you make visualization so real in your mind's eye that you can see, feel, and experience the very thing you wish to manifest in your world, your subconscious will have a solid blueprint upon which to build and program the dream experience into reality in whatever area of your life you choose.

The basis for a new worldwide shift to a greater understanding of and faith in the power of visualization lies in the belief that consciousness can transform energy into matter. When you embark on the tremendous journey of creating a perfect life for yourself through a vision of what you desire, be clear and exact in every respect.

I hear so many people scoff about anything to do with visualization. Some simply don't understand the concept. There are always the skeptics who decry anything they can't see, feel, or understand. I respect them—more because their skepticism allows the rest of us to go about our business of visualizing and creating largely unhindered.

Visualization is a primary tool of action and must be used correctly to see any positive results in your life. It should be practiced every day—the more often you create and hold the mental pictures in your mind, the more rapidly you reap the rewards. Practice every day (several times is recommended for empowerment) and you'll find it easier to hold the images for longer, thereby burning that new and inspired life onto your subconscious. This marks the beginning of that new reality.

Believe without reservation in what you want, dream it, visualize the successful outcome, and enact that plan of action. Shut out the fear and go for it. The results will amaze you.

I have always used creative visualization in one form or another. I know how difficult it is to manifest anything in your life if you can't visualize it.

I first paint a complete canvas in my mind before I even begin the process of bringing the image to life. If I'm unable to see something clearly in my mind, I know I will never be able to see it in my life.

On one such occasion, I dearly wanted to go to the US for a holiday. Friends were having a major celebration, and Suzannee and I were invited. I was booked to present a seminar on that particular weekend and so at that exact time we were unable to make the trip.

I truly wanted to be with my friends on that special occasion. I like nothing more than spending time in the company of fun people. I really love a party, so I was upset at the prospect of missing it. I decided I would somehow make the trip.

I began to visualize the journey in every minute detail. In my mind's eye I saw myself making the booking online; I had the confirmation in my hand. With our bags packed, we were standing in the check-in queue. We passed immigration, sat in the gate lounge, boarded the aircraft, and it took off.

I followed the entire journey in my mind, even to the point of attending the party of my friends. I went over it each night in every minute detail before I went to sleep and again in the morning during my meditation time.

Some weeks later (about six weeks before the celebration), the company asked me to reschedule the seminar to the following month. It came completely out of the blue. It turned out to be an amazing trip for Suzanne and me. It simply cemented the power of visualization in my mind.

Learn to use the power of creative visualization in specific manifestations. It's a tremendously potent tool for organizing thoughts into a logical and ordered pattern. Results can be amazing. You must remember to be focused, driven, and determined at all times. Accept as absolute your power to create a reality from your thoughts. You must believe without hesitation in your own ability, your creativity, and yourself.

We all possess immeasurable power within and need only understand the steps necessary to tap into that wealth of profound wisdom and unleash our incredible capacity for achievement.

I always sit and visualize what it is I want to achieve. I picture it in as much detail as possible. I see the object of my desire as precisely as I know it to be. I also give myself the freedom to alter the picture as circumstances change. It helps me to keep the mental picture real and relevant.

If you believe in the laws of the universe (and there are many), you'll understand them to be exact. There can be no room for doubt or misinterpretation.

Visualize, conceptualize, recognize, strategize, harmonize, realize, and materialize—you don't always have to rationalize.

No matter what it is you wish to achieve the creative visualization process will be greatly *enhanced* when you *can* make the image clear and precise. You have to truly believe in the power and validity of the images you're creating. Though they might at first lack clarity and depth, it stands to reason that with repeated visualization they inevitably become more vivid and real. Make the decision right here and now to be successful and abundant. Articulate your desires in the present tense and ensure your dreams and visions are in vivid color and clarity. Make them congruent with your actions so all aspects of your life are working in harmony.

Whatever questions you ask yourself, ensure the answers you give are powerful, driven, and, most importantly, in the present tense. See them in their entire splendor and enjoy the increasing feelings of euphoria as the reality of what you're doing begins to flood into your life. Avoid negativity at all costs and paint your mental images of success and prosperity with color and clarity. There can be no room for ambiguity.

Visualization allows you to go to that place where life is fantastic. It's a place where there's depth, wonder, and excitement. It offers incredibly bright sunshine with untapped abundance. It permits you to mold your ideal life around the opportunities presenting themselves (attracted by your positive and focused attitude). With practice it will soon become an absolute and indispensable constant in your new and inspired life.

> So many people spend precious time faking it through creating the illusion of success and abundance in their lives. They don't actually find the time, inclination, or courage to step from this false reality and make something of their existences.

Life is like a jigsaw puzzle. Very often we don't create a completed image of the end result, and we're unable to envisage what our future will look like. Other times we have the diagram, but it's incomplete. In both of these instances, we will struggle to develop the final picture.

There are other times when there might be pieces missing or we have items forced into wrong sections. In these instances too, we have an incomplete product and are unable to finish the puzzle.

However, when we have all the pieces together and possess the diagram—in full gloss color—we have a firm basis upon which to grow and develop a strong and optimistic future. It can take a lot of time and effort, but with focus and commitment we're able to emerge triumphantly.

To have a complete plan of your future and enable you to formulate a clear and vivid picture of the prize, you must possess *all* the pieces of the puzzle, fully intact. This is unfortunately a very rare situation when we begin our quest for a successful and abundant future. We generally strike out on the journey with an indistinct image of the finished product, and all too often we have pieces missing.

> Never allow uncertainty to divert you from your path to ultimate success. Believe in yourself, your journey, and your goal of an incredibly abundant future. Remain clear and focused.

Encouraging movement occurs in your life and goals begin to rapidly materialize when you have a powerful and deep-seated positive emotion attached to your images (see Chapter 10: "Change Your Habits, Change Your Life"). When they are constantly nourished with clear and results-driven mental pictures, you'll be presented with a powerful image of your desired life. Use the visualization process to elevate your subconscious power to create.

There will be times when a negative reaction to a situation can change your mind and shift your focus. The image you have of the future you seek could become faded and uncertain. This can also occur in those instances when you are impacted by pessimistic belief patterns.

Constant bombardment by the negative words, thoughts, actions, and emotions of others can have the same detrimental effect. The process happens at any age/time, and pressure on your feelings and emotions can cause you to revert to old habits. Negative belief patterns have to be un-learned and dismantled and new beliefs created and supported (see my previous book, *The Unstoppable Power Within*, Chapter 2: "The Essence of Self-Belief").

Comprehensive visualization comes from knowing, seeing, feeling, and embracing all we are and all we know we are capable of being, having, and achieving in our lives. That's an absolute understanding of precisely what we want and how we manifest it in spite of the obstacles faced.

Nothing incredible will occur in life without faith in the tasks we perform and a solid and immovable belief in our own ability to create exactly the life and future we desire.

Unless we can present the universe with a very distinct and clear picture of the future we want, we'll never achieve magnificent results. If we constantly change the image we have in our minds, we are presenting a distorted message of how we want our future to unfold.

You must create in your mind a very obvious representation, with total color and absolute certainty; there is no room for doubt. Through my coaching, I constantly mention the canvas of life. It requires a great deal of vivid color to remove any uncertainty. It's important to know beyond question what it is you truly desire. It helps maintain your focus, drive, and commitment.

With an understanding of this initial aspect of attraction, you can instigate the second and equally important component of the equation. In spite of what you may have been told or have been lead to believe, you actually have to put some effort into the task to realize a successful result. Affirmative Action is fundamental for any degree of success.

Once you decide to cease being ordinary, you've begun the journey to becoming extraordinary. It's in this truly magnificent state you achieve your next level of personal growth and development and find yourself on the paved road to becoming a true champion.

For instance, it makes no sense to plan for a great holiday—visualizing all the wonderful places you'll visit, people you may meet, things you can do—and excitedly discuss it with your family members and friends only to stay at home and miss the trip. The visualization amounts to nothing when you put no effort into realization. You must take *affirmative action*.

Know without doubt exactly what you want from and with your life, and put that plan of action in place today. Constantly refer to your vision to maintain your drive, commitment, and focus in your pursuit of an abundant future. This is where your Creation Board and journal are vitally important for the life, power, and clarity of and in your dreams. They assist in keeping alive those vivid images of a wonderful future.

> Once you have in your mind a clear and unconstrained vision of what you want and where you're going, it's time to take immediate action. The fundamental step to incredible success and abundance.

Seek everything you desire and have confidence in yourself, your visions, and that plan of action. Sitting around dreaming will not empower you. Wishing and hoping will not create anything worthwhile in your life; simply talking will never help your future materialize. Maintain the faith in yourself and all you desire. Never be self-limiting or believe anything other than the fact that you deserve great things in your life. Once you do this, take that affirmative action on your plan, and the wheels of destiny will begin to turn.

At some time in our lives, we've all used the power of creative visualization in one form or another, to manifest (or at the very least dream about) those things we most covet. It might be on the sporting field, in the class room, the office, or at home—perhaps while walking on the street or sitting on the bus (I never advocate doing this while driving/riding a vehicle; it's definitely a task on which to focus your full attention).

There's no question we do it in our sleep and during times of quiet contemplation. However, the ability to creatively visualize during waking moments is a learned process. The experience leaves you feeling refreshed and upbeat. The results can be amazing.

Every day of your existence, you make an impact on your life and your future. The manner in which you live your life communicates your intentions to your subconscious. It's not about how much material wealth you have, but in the way you walk, talk, and interact with other people. It's about how you think and the way you hold yourself. How you feel about your life and the positive and uplifting thoughts you hold in your mind about all aspects of your *Self* and your journey, other people and situations.

All components of your life work in harmony to build the world you want. Paramount to that equation is the way you think—it impacts on your inner being and gives you the thrust to begin and maintain a system of incredible transformation.

> Believe in yourself and know that you are always in the right place, at the right time, to meet the right people to fulfill your visions and dreams.

I have read much over the past twenty years on quantum physics and quantum theory. I initially had little idea of the importance of the information I was absorbing, nor the impact it was to have on my life all these years later.

A fundamental aspect of physics is the belief that our thoughts can and do affect us as individuals and, to a larger extent, the world at large. Scientists have concluded that when various experiments have been carried out, the thoughts of those conducting the experiments can and do impact the results obtained.

This information has lead scientists to believe that we do in fact have a direct impact on the world around us, where the power of our thoughts has the capacity to directly affect our reality.

I don't profess to fully understand the basis for and relationship between all matter in the universe. I have, however, begun to gain a more powerful understanding of my place in the here and now and the immense impact my thoughts, emotions, and creative visualization can have on my life, my future, and the world.

Even a basic understanding of quantum physics and quantum theory allows us to profoundly change the way we look at ourselves. They have certainly changed my life in incredible ways and given me a new and exciting perspective on just how I can challenge myself every day and direct my energy and focus to my ultimate destiny.

Never say "I can't." Always smile and see the beauty in every day. Take the time to talk to children. Love your family. Dream big and in color and always make time to smell the flowers along the way. Never complain when it rains—learn to dance or buy an umbrella. Keep the warmth in your heart and the fire in your belly. Remain focused and always look forward—destiny never walks behind you.

The way you interact with yourself is as fundamental as the interaction you have with the world around you. Each aspect of this development offers an impression of the person you are and wish to become. The way to evolve into the person you truly want to be is a system of complete, positive integration of your thoughts, words, and actions. The sooner you begin thinking and acting like the person you want to be, the sooner you will become that new and inspired individual.

Another important component of visualization is subliminal messaging. This is done where relaxing music is dubbed over positive and empowering words, phrases, and sentences. While you listen to the idyllic sounds, your mind is taking notice and reacting positively to the underlying messages.

Your positive thoughts and actions must be in total accord with your plans, wishes, and dreams. They work together as a system in unison. Anything that falls short will deliver a less than complete result. Remove the fractured and distorted images; make your dreams and visions clear and unmistakable.

It's easy to become disillusioned with some aspects of life where in many instances you've dreamed of something only to have it fail to materialize. You may also have your ideas shot down by others who are critical of your view on life and sarcastically accuse you of being a "dreamer."

I endured that negative impact for a great many years of my life through various relationships. It did deal a blow to my confidence and any immediate positive outcomes for my dreams, goals, and wishes. However, with experience and practice I pushed the negativity from my life, stripping it of all its power. With practice you too can prevail over this adversity.

Always ensure your internal porch light is illuminated. It throws out the welcome mat to attract a constant flow of goodness and opportunity into your existence.

When you begin to use your powers of visualization in a creative process, you'll encounter times when you're not totally focused and can become disillusioned with some of the outcomes. This will affect the way you view life and therefore impact your attitude. It completes a vicious circle of negativity.

Outwardly, you might project the image of a very focused and driven individual—very positive and forthright—though inwardly you continue to harbor those fears that hold you back and only serve to drive you further from your goals.

It's imperative to stay focused at all times, irrespective of the short term outcome of those ideas, plans, notions, and tasks you develop. You only give power to negativity if you continue to hold those images in your mind and don't replace them with positive and powerful thoughts and emotions.

While you give sanctuary to darkness and doubt, it will continue to manifest in your life irrespective of how many times you try and tell yourself you're on track. For instance, you will find it incredibly difficult to attract great things if you have niggling doubts and secretly harbor negative thoughts. Build absolute and unshakable faith in yourself and your ability, no matter what happens and in spite of the hurdles you encounter.

Feed your beliefs constantly and starve the doubts by reading inspirational material and talking with other like-minded individuals. Turn those whispers of doubt within to shouts of positive affirmation and give yourself every opportunity to realize your goals. You have to reward yourself with reasons to smile every day.

Your imagination is often a place you've only dreamed of visiting.

It's never too late to be successful. There is no time limit on turning your life around to become the person you truly want to be. Success and abundance begin with one dream, one notion, real passion, a clear vision and a solid plan of action. Today is the day that success begins to germinate in the life of someone. That person could be you, should be you, would be you if you'll finally make up your mind that abundance is to be your catch cry.

> Success is never confined to one language, culture, or religion. It doesn't entertain discrimination. It remains a special and all embracing, totally accessible universal gift.

If you have self-limiting beliefs, now is the time to change them into incredible power-driven, results-oriented forces. Have faith in yourself and your ability. Know beyond question that you are on the right path. Ensure your inside light is burning as brightly as it can to illuminate the path ahead and simultaneously attract great things to you.

If you have doubts or feelings of inadequacy, you're limiting your ability to grasp opportunities as they arise. They will become blinders shading you from what *could* be. Turn these into what *is* and what *will* be. Suddenly your absolute belief in what your magnificent future holds becomes the awesome power in the journey you're taking.

Unleash the courage, strength, and intestinal fortitude to succeed. The power of the future is absolute and lies deep within. Have that unerring belief in yourself and know you are on the right track. Believe that all you desire is truly possible and is continuing through this moment. Once you have faith in yourself and know you have a strong and committed plan for the future, there's no longer any room for doubt. Eliminate the darkness.

> Belief patterns act like windows to the future. If they remain negative, access to many opportunities will be restricted. Make them positive and results-driven; the window to success and abundance will open wide on all aspects of your incredible life.

Focus on specific goals and visions and they become a very concrete part of your psyche. You begin to live them, thereby giving them life and substance. Open your mind and allow the associated emotions to act like magnets and attract the various pieces of the puzzle you're creating. You'll slowly but surely begin to piece them together.

Creating this vision of your future is a crucial step toward building your reality. The more you practice, the more colorful and vivid the picture becomes and, therefore, the more real the dream. Constantly fire it with true passion for what you want and the deep-seated desire you have to create the ideal world for yourself.

Initially focus on what it is you desire. Be in the moment. See, feel, smell, taste, and live in and with the things you truly yearn. See the picture in full and vivid color. Know it is what you want. You should then ask for it—write it down in the present tense. In effect, you're creating a catalogue of great things in your life, fired with a true drive for and belief in exactly what it is you desire to fill your world and your power to create it.

The question will be answered in one form or another in time. The universe has a way of making things work—or rearranging your thoughts and requests and systematically manifesting them. The amount of time it takes is indeterminable. However, the more vivid you make your visualization and the more direct and colorful your writings, the more powerful will be your desires. At this level, the more likely you'll be to have your questions answered and your goals achieved.

Every great success begins with a clear and unambiguous visualization. Once you see it clearly in your mind, you will begin to see it as clearly in your life.

When you ask, you can release the question. If it has color, depth, and clarity and is covered in a thick layer of passion, sincerity, joy, and gratitude, it will reach the desired target. Get ready for the answer. Prepare yourself by living in the moment. Show true happiness and appreciation for the wonderful things you already enjoy and those you know beyond question will come into your life.

A positive mental imprint is 100 times more powerful than a negative thought. I believe that to be the absolute truth because I'm so blessed every day in my life.

Emotions are our way of truly understanding and appreciating what we're attracting. Sometimes, however, we let them get in the way of our positive thought processes. We can too easily allow them to push our positive thoughts to one side.

What you're feeling can and should be a reflection of the positive things which are occurring in your life. It must also support exactly what you're in the process of attracting. When you fill your life with happiness and gratitude for what you have, you're creating a very positive and effective doorway through which your visualization can deliver your wishes. Occupy your every space with warm, loving, and compassionate feelings. The universe will always respond.

As you seek love, peace, happiness, success, good health, and prosperity in your own life, also wish it unconditionally in the lives of every other person.

Imagine just how powerful that notion would become if every person on the planet wished for goodness, success, and happiness for all others. The world would be an awesome place.

Become attuned to your feelings and emotions and refrain from maintaining unrealistic expectations for the outcome of any particular circumstances. It automatically depletes a situation of joy and passion and runs the risk of becoming rigid and stagnant.

This is true too of happiness, where we often inadvertently set ourselves up for a punishing ride with a specific expectation for fulfillment of our wishes and desires. It takes our focus away from the eventual prize and removes us from our natural progression.

> You can't taste or touch it, neither can you drive or drink it. You can't hold or hoard it. You can't borrow or buy it. Success is something you choose to have in your life, and from that moment on it will begin to manifest itself in many wonderful ways.

Life's journey should involve a great deal of give and take. Rather than insisting that it's "your way or the highway," appreciate the need to listen to others and have a broad and colorful view of the world. It's not the end of existence as we know it if we're ever wrong; listening to others often helps us understand much more about ourselves and realign our belief patterns.

Whatever is occurring in your life can be changed with a shift in your consciousness. If you have negative feelings at any particular time, this will impact on what is occurring around you. Shift those feelings to be positive, and the effects can be profound.

> Never cry for the things you can't change. Instead, have joy and gratitude for those you can.

Remaining positive can at times prove to be a difficult process. During those periods where the going gets a little tough, you can so easily revert to old, comfortable and "safe" habits. It's times like these when you'll have the tendency to lose focus. No matter who you are, it's not possible to control every situation. It is counter-productive to a constructive mindset and serves no positive purpose. You will inevitably be fighting a losing battle.

When you fall into the habit of focusing on what you *don't want*, you find those very things begin to manifest because it's on these you focus your full attention. Therefore it makes a great deal of sense to center your attention on what you *do* want—those more positive and uplifting things with the capacity to bring joy, happiness, love, and abundance into your life.

Always go with your feelings and allow your heart to provide a road map. Use your left brain (logic, detail, and facts) to set out your plan, supervised by your right brain (feelings, imagination, and creativity) in unison with your heart.

Guide your journey with a warmth and light from that special place within. Give yourself permission to bask in the glow of your successes with the freedom to accept momentary errors of judgment. They too are a fact of life.

Look on positive thoughts as true gifts. Fully embrace them because they offer us the opportunity to master our own destinies. They encourage us to take action to bring warmth, good health, love, happiness, success, abundance, and prosperity into our lives and encourage others to do the same.

> To experience success and abundance in my life, I need to see, feel, hear, taste, and experience it in the here and now.

Those who lack success and prosperity in their lives communicate this in all they do. Others who have a rich and plentiful life and are confident with the direction they're taking speak this positive energy in every aspect of their interaction within their communities.

Have you ever noticed how a room lights up when a particular person enters? The individual appears to radiate an inner glow that instantly draws others to what exhibits as genuine and all-encompassing warmth. It transcends simple looks and personality. You may even be one of those fortunate people in whose company others seek to be.

These are the individuals who display what is often termed the "it factor," or that special something that makes them stand out above the crowd. It's the entire package and can't be explained by one simple aspect of that person's makeup. It shines from within and, like a magnet, draws others into the circle.

> Within twenty-four hours, today will become simply a page in history. Ensure it reads like a roadmap to success.

There's no doubt many elements in our existence affect consciousness. Everything we encounter in our daily lives will impact our belief patterns on many things, including wealth and success. A disorganized and untidy daily life will add to the often deep-rooted feelings of lethargy and inadequacy we hold about ourselves and our existences. If we have a dilapidated vehicle; if the house requires painting or the roof is leaking, cupboards brimming, and rubbish bins are overflowing; where clothes are strewn across the floor or the yard is overgrown. All this simply exacerbates the feelings of emptiness and widens the chasm in our worlds.

When you have signs and elements of negativity in your life and you make no conscious effort to eliminate or replace them (with positive factors of course), then you are building an air of pessimism around you and indicating your willingness to reside happily in that oppressive state. Complaining only adds to the impact of the negativity. It's not enough to simply think about improvements and pine for something different. You actually have to take action.

> When you feel good about yourself and your life, where your environment reflects these powerful and uplifting emotions, it has a habit of attracting positive energy into your world.

Make the conscious effort to improve your life. Do something positive to give yourself further reasons to feel good about the brilliant existence you know you can lead. Nothing is out of reach if you only have faith in yourself and understand that you are capable of having anything you want. Believe it beyond all doubt.

The many complimenting and competing elements in your environment will in some way affect you. Everything you see and experience will subconsciously impress upon the ideas you hold in relation to wealth, health, and happiness. The more broken and decaying articles you gather around you without replacing them, the greater will be your feelings of abject frustration. The more you clutter your house with "useless" things, the less room you have for growth and empowerment. Unchecked rubbish about the office and home is also a real block to successful thinking.

These negative actions signal to the universe your willingness to accept second best in all aspects of your life and, therefore, an unwillingness to grasp opportunities and progress.

When you keep signs of abundance in your environment, your subconscious mind is constantly impressed with the idea of wealth—visualizing it on a daily basis. In the world of cause and effect, the notion of abundance as a constant in your life, allows you to enable that very condition.

> The bigger the dream, the greater the vision, the more real the outcome, the more breathtaking the success.

If you want to be a millionaire, a sports champion, an award-winning artist, racing car driver, successful entrepreneur or teacher, it's quite simple—*start thinking like one.* Begin a program where you study the habits of successful people and understand what makes them tick and how they develop their incredibly steely mindset of success and abundance. Attend conferences and seminars and gather material to strengthen your focus on great wealth and prosperity. If necessary, enlist the services of a coach/mentor to help fire your passions, channel your thoughts and actions, and point you in the right direction. Perhaps you might embark on a course of appropriate study. Do whatever is necessary to realize your ambition.

Use this attitude in all aspects of your creative visualization. See yourself in the moment doing the thing you want. Gather your information on the various people whose success you wish to emulate. Make it part of your everyday actions. Begin to feel and act as a successful person might. I never suggest you commence spending loads of money, especially when you don't have it. This is a negative step and quite reckless. It can only serve to sabotage your efforts and set you back. At all costs, refrain from faking it until you make it. That is one of the most destructive courses of action you can take. It can derail your efforts and keep you from ever achieving your dreams.

Having and acknowledging abundance in one or more areas of your life enables you to reprogram your conditioning. You begin to see and feel increasing prosperity across all areas of your world. Identify those instances in your life where you experience euphoria through feelings of happiness and increased wealth and abundance. Slowly but consciously begin to create many more of them.

In essence, continue to generate aspects where these feelings of success are becoming more pronounced. It enables you to impress on your subconscious those things that can start to become norms in your everyday life.

> The most precious gift we hold is the ability to recognize and explore our own opportunities with courage, self-respect, passion, vision, persistence, and above all, love and gratitude.

Creative visualization is more than simply closing your eyes and thinking of something great. Dreaming of a sports car, holiday overseas, or a new girlfriend won't make anything magically appear. That would take all the fun out of the personal development aspect of life; the ability and opportunity to seize success and abundance would be greatly diminished.

There is a special set of steps you take in the overall process. You have to do more than simply think about something. It has to occupy your psyche—become part of your life as you live and breathe your new existence. You have to truly grasp the experience. That means *you must take action*.

It's not always possible to find a quiet place and concentrate on those innermost thoughts. However, you can do it at any time of the night and day. (Many call it daydreaming; I call it success creation.) Make it simple to start with and build on the images as you create them.

Whatever you want, visualize yourself experiencing the feel, smell, taste, and touch. Use color and substance in your visualization. Give it mass and character. If it's a new car, smell the leather, feel the grip of the steering wheel and the roar of the engine. Feel the wind in your hair with the top down. See the admiring glances from the passers-by. Feel the hum as you smoothly change gears. *See* yourself as the proud owner of this great new set of wheels.

What you think and the way you feel about yourself will ultimately dictate the impression you leave on others.

Similarly, see the wonderful brickwork of your new house with the home cinema and gym, games room, landscaped gardens, pool, tennis court, and tree-lined driveway. Your enthusiasm and passion are endless; so too are the opportunities in your life and your ability to create them.

You express your respect for yourself and confirm your belief in your own magnificence through behaving in a manner indicative of the admiration you hold for yourself and the regard you have for your hierarchy of values.

You add new dimensions to your life and build strong and substantial foundations for your future every day through the quality of the friendships you cherish; the happiness and gratitude you put in your life; the eminence you build in all your dealings with others; and the drive, vision, and focus you have for a greater and more respectful existence. These are all indications to your subconscious mind of the type of person you are and wish to be and the existence you truly want to embrace.

Begin this incredible process of transformation in the way you live your everyday life. If you seek wealth, happiness, and abundance, live your life *now* as if you are already healthy, wealthy, and abundant. Live in a way that makes you truly happy. It doesn't mean you should ever live beyond your means because that behavior can lead to doom and gloom.

When you feel you have to live extravagantly or make an (unnecessary) impression on others, it's an indication of your lack of belief in yourself and your failure to live a happy and fulfilled existence. It indicates your inability to envisage yourself as an empowered and enriched individual and can only impact negatively on your life and the lives of those around you.

Being successful and abundant is not about another person's perspective of your life. In fact, it's a reflection of the love and respect you have for yourself in all aspects of your existence. The positive impact you have on others and your environment should resonate with your highest values so you begin to vibrate with your visions of happiness, success, prosperity, and good health.

> Never underestimate the power you hold inside to affect every area of your existence. Believe it to be so and just do it.

Commence the process of taking your dreams from a surreal state into reality by mentally putting yourself in that situation. You support this through your plan of action and the determination to see it through. You must truly believe in yourself and the life you're living. Visualize yourself doing those things *now* and enjoy every aspect of your world. Remain upbeat and passionate about your life and the direction you're traveling. Don't allow negativity to block your vision, and never permit others to steal your dream or overshadow your view of the future.

Nothing will simply materialize without a plan and the steely determination to realize it. To become a reality, a dream requires sustained action. It necessitates positive and concrete steps to achieve the desired result. When you visualize what you want, you systematically build on your dreams through the process of creating the strong platform required to support all you desire. Your plan of action is your launching pad from that foundation.

Creative visualization is a very real part of wealth creation. It enables you to remain focused and build your ideal life. Once you have the images of this wonderful existence in your mind, keep them vibrant and spend time molding, coloring, and developing them into a powerful platform from which to launch your plan.

> Good intentions will never amount to great accomplishments until you realize that vision and persistence are the driving forces required to make dreams a reality. Success and abundance will continue to elude you until you realize and appreciate the relationship.

Begin with small steps to experience the extraordinary impact your thoughts and subsequent actions will have on your life. It becomes easier to hold predominantly positive thoughts in our minds when we continue to build our thoughts and emotions on optimistic issues and move to eliminate the negativity that impacts us. Constantly reinforce your importance and relevance in the moment.

Make your questions strong and focused to have the greatest impact. It provides your mind with something powerful to search for. According to Noah St. John, "When your sub-conscious is given a question, it sets about finding a plausible answer."[1] I've been using this technique with great success for some considerable time.

The use of positive affirmations is an integral part of this powerful process. You should put yourself squarely in the moment using the "Why am I" principle:

- Why am I so happy, healthy, and prosperous?
- Why am I such a successful and empowered person?
- Why am I an individual to whom opportunity comes easily?
- Why am I so incredibly abundant in all areas of my life?
- Why am I such a successful and prosperous entrepreneur?
- Why am I a person who gives love unconditionally and is loved by my family and friends?

Instead of a string of invectives when you become angry and frustrated, condition yourself to clear the fog of indecision and inaction. Use positive and creative terms to describe yourself, your life, and the current conditions, no matter what obstacles stand in your way.

When you replace negative thoughts with more positive affirmations, you'll begin to experience some incredible changes in your life. Believe unreservedly in yourself and your plan and have faith in the person you are and are becoming. It's not enough to occasionally think positive thoughts and hope that things will turn out alright. Neither is it beneficial to your long-term plans for success if you simply wander through life giving occasional thought to what you are capable of achieving.

Build the journey of your life in your mind one stone at a time, and show gratitude for all that's assisting you to fulfill your dreams. Keep the warmth, energy, color, and clarity in every aspect of the picture. Continue the fruitful process of creating the ideal life for yourself and your family.

> Gratitude is not a burden, nor is it a reason to cultivate self-doubt. It represents a purpose for striving for greater opportunities in life.

If you are unable to visualize your ideal life, I can almost guarantee you will be unable to realize it. Effort and commitment are required each day to open your channels to success and abundance. Don't look on it as a chore, but rather as a prelude to greater things to come.

Train yourself to rise early and find a quiet place (it's often difficult when you have specific things to do or children/family members who require attention). Alternatively, you might prefer some quiet time last thing of an evening, just before you fall into a deep and relaxing sleep. Try to set aside just fifteen minutes, morning and/or evening. With practice, it can also be done as you walk or travel on public transport to work or study or during your daily exercise routine (once again, never practice it while driving or riding—the results could be fatal!).

Research indicates that the Alpha state of the mind provides the ideal platform for learning. The brain is relaxed, focused, and aware and runs at about 8 to 12 cycles per second (Hertz) and is generally associated with right brain activity.[2]

We're also reminded that the Alpha state offers a host of incredible benefits. These include a heightened awareness and increases in levels of creativity, improvements in sleep patterns, personal health, and general feelings of wellbeing.

In the Beta (normal waking) state the brain runs about 13 to 30 Hertz. This is more closely aligned with left brain activity. This pattern is strongly associated with perception and consciousness. Researchers believe Gamma waves (many class these under Beta waves) are present on a continuous basis during low voltage, fast neocortical activity occurring during waking and active rapid eye movement (REM).[3]

The other states are referred to as Theta or deeper relaxation (4 to 7 cycles per second), a subconscious to super-conscious state, a condition of high creation, and the sleep state. This is related to the right brain.[4] The last is the Delta or unconscious/super-conscious state (.5 to 3.5 Hertz). It is the ideal level for healing or rejuvenation.[5]

> Once you allow yourself to go within, you will believe in yourself as a wonderful and unique being. Listen to your inner voice, and your subconscious self will surely lead you to personal greatness in your life.

Those oft referred to "aha" moments occur in the Alpha state—a period of high alert where profound and impacting thoughts and ideas happen. There are many great leaders and thinkers who would have been in an Alpha state when they hit on those brilliant, life-altering ideas that literally changed the way we live? Think of Alexander Graham Bell, John Logie Baird, Ralph H. Baer, Benjamin Franklin, Wilbur and Orville Wright, Thomas Edison, Ladislo Biro, and even Bill Gates—they're just a few of history's most successful creators.

There is a variety of ways to achieve this serene state of relaxation. These include meditation exercises, playing certain forms/styles of music, yoga, subliminal messaging, biofeedback (response to specific stimuli), and various breathing techniques.

I've used several of these techniques with much success. Wherever possible, do it last thing at night or first thing in the morning, when the mind is alert and relaxed. I have also on occasions combined meditation, breathing, and a floatation tank to put myself into an incredible state of complete relaxation with outstanding results. The mind is free to wander, search, question and create. I even use the bath at night with candles nearby and soft and soothing music to create an atmosphere conducive to total respite.

> There is a difference between dreaming of something and having a dream. Once you embrace the difference, your focus will shift and success and abundance will begin to materialize.

For the benefit of this exercise, I shall concentrate on the simple act of breathing to assist in attaining effective results. You require no outside stimuli or tools. You can then move on to combining the technique with others as outlined in preceding paragraphs. There is much information available on the Internet to assist in this powerful process of personal and spiritual development.

Close your eyes and take ten slow deep breaths—in through the nose and out through the mouth. Become completely relaxed. The process helps you achieve an Alpha state. Clear your mind and hear only the rhythm of your breathing. The more you do it, the greater and more finely tuned will be your focus.

To commence the process of visualization, begin by picturing yourself in a favorite place. Perhaps that's the beach, in a park, or under the stars. It might be with a loved one or spending time with a pet.

Continue your deep breaths and feel the total relaxation flood over your body as your brain enters the Alpha state. Your mind will begin to clear and your focus become sharp.

Once relaxed and composed, begin filling your mind with the many creative images you wish to manifest. It is paramount you do your very best to exclude distracting thoughts and emotions from your mind. Concentrate only on the positive aspects of your intended manifestations. This will become much easier with practice.

Apply your full attention to something you truly want in your life. Picture yourself doing or receiving that exact thing, whether it's meeting someone special, receiving an award, or achieving an exceptional outcome for a project. Make the picture vivid and in full color. Begin the process today.

> When you fill your day with positive and results-driven affirmations, you're creating a strong and long lasting platform for success.

Constantly feed your mind with affirmative, life-changing thoughts, emotions, actions, and images. As far as possible, absorb only positive, "good health" material to keep you focused and stimulated. Take steps to keep away from negative information and influences. They only serve to bring you down where you run the very real risk of becoming derailed from your vision and ultimately your purpose.

Fill every night and day with those affirmative thoughts, words, and pictures. They will assist you to remain more positive and uplifted about the things in life that truly matter. It also reinforces your capacity to manifest the ideal existence in spite of the occasional negative thought that might from time to time creep into your psyche. Try and make this positive emphasis a substantial part of your everyday life.

Visualize the optimistic outcome of the action. Picture yourself in the moment. It's you, it's what you want, and it's now. Continue your breathing—in through the nose and out through the mouth—continue your mental creativity.

Feel this wonderful experience. You are the very person you love, respect, and admire. You are a wonderful, creative, abundant, and happy individual living the ideal life. Allow your senses to pass through every aspect of the fantastic time and fully embrace it. See it clearly; live it in your mind. Hold close the emotions invoked and feel the warmth. Experience the cheers, the laughs, and even the tears of joy.

> Creative visualization is a powerful and indispensable tool to take your dreams from your subconscious into the bright, warm light of reality.

In adopting the visualization process for at least fifteen minutes every day (as often as possible), you're making that very clear link with the universe. You're also signaling your intention to find something more powerful and enriching in your life. It's an enormous step toward eliminating doubt and procrastination from your world and manifesting those things you most desire.

I go through my meditations for at least thirty minutes each day because I place high value on the desired outcomes. I spend an hour in a meditative state on those days when I feel the need for extra cleansing and a boost to the positive thoughts and images. Wherever possible, I combine my meditation with exercise that includes a long run by the water with some soothing music.

It takes some very powerful steps to move the dreamscape into a state of reality. This gives life, color, clarity, scope, and power to your visions, desires, and wishes. It will soon become second nature in your arsenal of tools and evolve into a mandatory assistant.

> The power of your dreams can catapult you to incredible success and abundance. Never underestimate the unfathomable value of visualization.

Combine this with your declarations of gratitude every day, and your life will take on a whole new meaning. While carrying out an exercise beneficial to your health and wellbeing, you're also creating the very existence you want. Combined with your plan of action and steely determination, your life will begin to change in extraordinary ways.

When the goal becomes crystal clear in your mind, it will begin to take shape in your reality. Ensure your images are strong, positive, and success-friendly. Whatever you focus your attention on (including the negatives) has the capacity to manifest in your life.

Welcome these warm and attractive positive images every time you use the visualization process. Should your thoughts occasionally wander to any negative things impacting your life, you run the risk of overshadowing and counteracting the constructive thought patterns you are creating.

I combine the breathing exercises with my Creation Board (see the next chapter) as an accessible and effective everyday tool to assist me to retain (and sometimes regain) my focus and stay on track. It's a wonderful device for keeping my dreams alive.

Make your journal a "revered repository" for all your dreams and desires. Add the descriptive pictures and words. Be as big and as bold as you wish and use it every day to remind you of how magnificent you are, how truly wonderful your life is, and how amazing your future is becoming.

NOTES

1. See his program, available at http://www.noahstjohn.com/try-afformations/.

2. Symphonic Mind Ltd., "What Are Brainwaves?" BrainWorks, Alpha Waves, accessed February 15, 2015, http://www.brainworksneurotherapy.com/what-are-brainwaves.

3. Ibid., Beta Waves.

4. Ibid., Theta Waves.

5. Ibid., Delta Waves.

If you dream you can, think you can, know you can, and accept nothing but success in your life, then you will.

LESSONS LEARNED

1. We all use creative visualization in our lives, every day.

2. Creative visualization helps to build reality.

3. The more you practice creative visualization, the more colorful and vivid the images will become.

4. The way you feel about yourself has a profound effect on your life.

5. When you feel good about yourself and your life, you can literally light up a room.

6. Believe in your dreams and goals to breathe life and substance into them.

7. Keep your creative images at the forefront of your mind to give them life and color.

8. Give yourself reasons every day to feel good about yourself and your life.

9. The step from ordinary to extraordinary is to believe in yourself and your plan.

10. If you can visualize it, you can realize it.

11. In the Alpha state is where your "aha" moments take place.

12. Constantly feed your mind with positive, life-changing thoughts and images.

13. Visualize yourself as the exact person you expect to be.

14. Your Creation Board is a great tool in assisting creative visualization.

15. Allow your Creation Board to remind you how magnificent you and your life are.

Chapter 4

YOUR INDISPENSABLE CREATION BOARD

The flaws of yesterday can only affect tomorrow if I anchor myself in the past. I must allow my future to have a strong foundation based on my dreams and visions created today.

The idea of a Creation Board came to me in the late 1980s when I found myself searching for something—some light and power—to push me forward in my relentless pursuit of enlightenment. I believe we all have a function in life—a purpose—we need only recognize and support that principle and we can begin to see more clearly the opportunities as they arise in our daily lives.

It was shortly after the birth of my beautiful son Kayle. I was sitting on the back step of my home writing and daydreaming (*success creating*) as a usual component of my day. I looked up to see a beautiful rainbow across the sky. It was incredibly vivid and the colors began to swirl in front of my eyes.

The image relaxed me, and I began to feel completely at ease. I realized the image was inducing an almost involuntary meditative response. The idea of constructing my "Board of Creation" was born. That evening, I made my first prototype.

> Constantly flood your mind with all the color, clarity, and splendor of your ideal life. It will soon become an integral part of your existence.

It was initially small—about 12 by 6 inches—and stood on my desk. It was made of cork and carried a simple collection of wonderfully uplifting words and empowering pictures. I looked at it every day when I was writing and creating at my computer (and of course my diary). I gained enormous drive, clarity, and focus from this very humble but incredibly empowering tool. I also began to carry pictures and inspiring phrases in my wallet.

Through a belief in myself and my ability, I realized I had at last found my calling: To assist others achieve their goals through a realization of their own true magnificence. There is no doubt life is often a rollercoaster ride. However, it can eventually lead to an incredible place of enlightenment. The struggles, trials, and tribulations; the turmoil, heartache, and pain were (and are) all part of that journey.

> Every time you envisage personal success and take affirmative action to achieve it, you move one step closer to your destiny.

An important aspect of personal and professional development is the ability and willingness to recognize our own shortcomings. Once we can do that without judgment, we're also able to realize and appreciate our strengths. We discover the courage to stand up each time we're knocked down and systematically build a life of which we can be exceedingly proud.

This is exhilarating and powerful. It can also be a sometimes long and arduous journey. It presents the evolution of that deep seated self-belief—the courage and determination to capitalize on all we are and everything we strive to be. It creates in us the drive to get back up and fight for the right to be successful in spite of the challenges we face. This is a basic human right and remains one of the fundamental keys to prosperity.

When we use a personalized board with our own unique dreams and goals on it, we are heading in the right direction; to a wonderful life of our own making. It's a common thread to assist every one of us to achieve all we desire. When we're working with drive and focus toward an optimistic and passionate outcome, the atmosphere is charged with incredibly positive energy.

Success and abundance are at the very heart of the dreams of each and every one of us. Because we're all linked, we share a joint destiny—to be the best and most successful we can.

> Use the words and beliefs of others only where they parallel your own. Once you have your clear vision of your destiny, let it be your one true navigator.

I have no doubt my Creation Board has assisted me to find and maintain a strong and focused direction in life. Combined with affirmations, it has the capacity to alter the thought patterns of anyone who has the determination and passion for something inspiring and enlightening in life—perhaps a new and inspiring direction. It can bring a life back on track (and keep it there). It has the ability to lead to some really amazing places.

I'm convinced the Creation Board will become an integral part of your everyday life as you search for and embrace change. It works quietly but consistently on the mind, assisting in the pursuit of personal success and abundance. It continues to work for me, 24 hours of each day; every week, month, and year.

Your Creation Board enables you to highlight, in pictures and words, the brilliant story you are already establishing. It concerns your dreams, visions, and goals. It outlines where you want to go, the person you are evolving into, and what you are achieving. Focus your mind on the wonderful words and images each day and begin to program yourself for the truly abundant world awaiting your arrival.

Life is composed of a series of journeys to a variety of destinations throughout our existence. Once we arrive at one, we immediately set sail for another.

That's the beauty of success creation. It gives us something to look forward to and invokes tangible images and visions into which we can put our energy and drive. The more progress we make, the more empowered and inspired we become.

> When you decide on your destination, the type of journey you wish to take, and the amount of abundance, color, and passion you want to fill every day—dream it, see it, plan it, and go for it.

The more often you exercise your visualization processes (ideally, a meaningful habit at least fifteen to thirty minutes each day), the easier and more profound it will become. Train your mind to be in tune with everything you envisage for your future. It becomes an inevitable part of your reality. The drive and momentum will constantly sustain you.

There are primarily three styles of Creation Board. The first is the stationary (board) type hanging on your wall or sitting on your desk. It holds all your dreams, visions, and emotions. It can be any size, though I suggest something of a reasonable size—about 24 by 36 inches for the wall and 12 by 12 inches for the desk.

Pin pictures on it and write uplifting words and phrases to describe your ideal life. Spend quality time examining the wonderful creativity; drink in all the power, color, and emotion of the ideal life you're creating. Live the story you've created upon it. Begin to see it clearly in your mind's eye.

The second type is a screensaver on your computer. It offers a vivid and moving representation of your life. Every day it's a constant reminder of your wonderful and empowering journey.

The third is an electronic device holding uploaded words and images. Once again it can stand on the desk or hang on the wall. You can take it with you as a constant reminder when traveling. I have all three and use them every day to build my ideal life and continue the journey to fulfillment.

> Before you tell yourself you can't do something, stop and picture how it will make you feel when you actually achieve it.

Give life to your Creation Board by making drawings, adding pictures, and communicating your desires in colorful and passionate expressions. Construct stories with pictures depicting yourself where you ideally want to be—with a loving companion; in that great job; with the shiny new sports car or the big house; enjoying a very prosperous, healthy, and contented lifestyle.

Superimpose pictures of yourself in whatever situation you wish—in the car, the new house, with friends, or sitting in the business class airline seat (before you download or copy information from any source, ensure you don't breach any copyright laws).

> Your imagination sets your future in motion. Make it colorful; make it powerful; make it count for something exceptional.

My Creation Board is full of graphic, color images and demonstrative words. They make up my future as I see it unfolding. It includes pictures of myself with those influential people I know beyond question are part of my incredible destiny. I have words and images to evoke significant emotions about my feelings for the brilliant life I know is unfolding through my dreams, visions, plans, drive, and optimism.

Every day you procrastinate is a setback to your future success and abundance. Create the reality you want *right now*. Each time you look at your Creation Board, be determined about the life you truly desire. Every time you close your eyes or take the time to look inside yourself, know you're heading in the right direction. In doing that, envisage your future in all its magnificence.

> Once you open your mind and your heart, the color of life will touch every corner of your being and lead you on a fantastic journey of discovery.

Modify your display at any time depending upon circumstances and opportunities arising along the way. Ensure you're in a sound and happy state of mind when you make those changes. That way, you'll make positive and effective modifications and remain focused and on track.

Negative thoughts and emotions will have the capacity to adversely impact your vision in the moment and, therefore, contrast with your otherwise happy, positive, and upbeat feelings. These could serve to temporarily derail you from your purpose.

Put anything you want on your Creation Board relating to your plan of action, your desired destination, where you see yourself and your life, and how you feel about your world. Include the income you know you deserve from your great new job, the house you intend to live in, and the car you'll drive. Support it with corresponding pictures in full and vivid color (even images of checks and bank deposit slips).

> Opportunity grows out of a personal drive and vision for something greater in our lives. It should therefore only be offered optimism, honesty, skill, talent, performance, and gratitude.

Put yourself in the moment and insert yourself in those wonderful and uplifting pictures. Visualize yourself enjoying those things *right now*. Take pleasure in the happy feelings and emotions, and know beyond doubt you deserve great things in your life at this very moment. Make sure your plan of action is in harmony with your dreams and goals, and work diligently and confidently toward them.

Constantly look at your Creation Board and remind yourself that success and abundance are rights—they are certainly not privileges reserved for a few fortunate individuals. Be confident of your ability to sustain that journey and embrace your right to possess great things. Use your Creation Board as part of your ongoing materialization processes and support it with the exercises discussed previously in Chapter 3.

Continue to develop your plan of action. Retain your unyielding focus on the goal ahead. It's a very real pot of gold you create at the end of the rainbow on your own personal journey to success and abundance. You relentlessly pursue, encourage, and welcome it in spite of trials and tribulations that can (and more than likely will) confront you.

Look at your Creation Board every day. Drink in its value to your life, purpose, and future. Make additions as your world evolves and success grows over time. Don't be afraid to make appropriate modifications during those times of need. As your vision, dreams, and plans change, so too will the contents of your Creation Board.

꿍

If the journey of life appears daunting, remember you only reach your destination by taking one step at a time.

Believe in yourself and your ability. Success occurs when we invite it into our lives. We make the conscious decision to initiate positive and life-altering amendments to the way we see and feel about our existence. In spite of what might be impacting us, it's important keep the focus and positive attitude.

Begin the incredibly stimulating process of attracting great things into your world right now. There's no time like the present to turn your life around. Have unerring faith in yourself and your ability, and allow nothing to deter you from your path.

Take the initiative; when necessary, permit your life to take a radical and exceptional turn for the better. Allow your Creation Board to be a critical component of your success strategy. Once you take that step into the empowering world of self-fulfillment, you notice the changes almost immediately. Your life begins to grow and flourish under the new conditions you've created.

Decide today to be all you know you can. Create and live the life you know you deserve. Open your mind and your heart to all that's possible. Don't waste time lamenting the past and all its hurdles and hiccups. There's no longer any such thing as *what could have been*, only *what can be*. It's now up to you.

You are who you are and where you are right now because of your vision, effort, and persistence. If you're not who or where you'd like to be, you need to believe in yourself and fuel your journey. It's never too late to succeed.

LESSONS LEARNED

1. Build your Creation Board in words and pictures for the exact life you desire.

2. Create your own personal journey to the pot of gold at the end of the rainbow.

3. Make your Creation Board colorful and expressive of your dreams and desires.

4. Always put yourself in the moment.

5. Success and abundance are rights, not privileges.

6. Remain confident and fully embrace your right to great things.

7. Look beyond the trials and tribulations and remind yourself of your goals every day.

8. Always believe in yourself and your ability to create, develop, and succeed.

9. Turn your life around by inviting success and abundance into your world.

10. Decide today to achieve everything that's possible in your life.

11. Always approach life with an open mind and compassionate heart.

Chapter 5

YOUR MANDATORY
DIARY/JOURNAL

How will history write your epitaph? Are you the person
with commitment and determination, who takes a chance
and is unafraid to try and perhaps occasionally fail? Or,
are you someone who only watches safely from the
sideline as the game of life passes before your eyes?

I've written personal inspirational quotations for most of my life and stored
them away in notepads, books, boxes, drawers, and journals. My first memory
as an inspirational writer is as a timid youngster (seven years old), sitting on the
veranda of my aunt's country home, writing in a book, with her wonderful old
dog Rover (believe it or not) at my side. I was in quiet contemplation, looking
across the front yard to the river nearby. It was a wonderful place where I spent
much of my childhood. The house was warm and inviting, and the river seemed
to hypnotize me. I was always in a creative mood when I visited that happy place.

I still do it to this day (write, that is, not sit with Rover. He died a long
time ago!). I find it a real source of inspiration and stimulation. It's a fundamental aspect of growth and development, and a great way to focus my energy
and drive in the direction I continue to travel.

Of course, now I write in my journal but transcribe those ideas, notions, and thoughts to my computer. It helps to enhance my daily existence and breathe life into my world (I also back up the material—imperative for all information on the computer; I even back up the backup).

I began the natural progression from the thinking and creating process to recording my thoughts. They're born from a need to understand what's going on around me and to focus my energy and drive on the life I truly want. It has become the ideal way to exercise my creativity.

> Always look at life first with your heart, then your eyes and your mind. Don't allow prejudice, doubt, or fear to overshadow your creativity, drive, vision, and eventual success.

Very early in life, these flashes of inspiration came to me at all times of the day and night. Initially I felt like a dilettante—not really understanding why I was writing but feeling the need to do so. I didn't really understand; but rather than disregard them as mere thoughts, I began gathering them together. I believed I was receiving the messages for a reason. They continue to come into my life on a daily basis. I consider the concept a crucial part of my spiritual development.

Receiving these inspirational thoughts enables me to remain on track when I feel uncertainty creeping into my mind. I now combine my writing with what I call times of *living in the moment*. I hold the important images in my mind as often and for as long as I can. It's living in the here and now to imprint indelibly on my mind the life I truly want and I believe I deserve. Doing this consistently influences my state of mind and it opens new doors. It creates a true atmosphere of positive energy and focuses my thoughts and emotions squarely on my dreams and goals. I've done it for new business enterprises, lottery tickets, travel, accommodation, parking spaces, and even the purchase of a new home and car!

Your diary can be a true lifeline, a safe haven where you record all your dreams, goals, visions, wishes, plans, hopes, deepest thoughts, and desires. It can impact your future in a very positive way. It becomes an ideal storehouse for your ideas and those "flashes" which come, often out of the blue. They can become accelerators for your drive for success as you put them into play. You can also systematically revise them as the need arises.

> If you leave success to chance, it might never have life. Decide today to bring it into your world and you give it power and direction.

These powerful writings act as visual prompts in those times when you have mind blocks. They become precise (and precious) records for any future marketing and sales strategies, and they stand as historical records of your transition to an abundant life.

If you every find yourself on the threshold of something but you're unsure of the next step, take the time to think about your situation and have gratitude for the new direction you're traveling.

One day I found I was locked out of the house. I sat on the step, thinking how I might get inside. I was thinking deeply when a light seemed to go on in my head. I began to understand the missing elements in my life. I realized there were certain things I needed to do so I could fully and absolutely embrace success.

In those moments I realized I required a key to open the door separating me from my goals. I was convinced it would provide a link to the tools necessary to realize a brighter future. I knew my life was changing in some extraordinary ways, and I was really empowered in those moments of realization (for those interested, I did get inside the house when I located a closed but unlocked window!).

With a great new attitude, focus, and a renewed enthusiasm, I uncovered that priceless little gem—something to inspire me and give me the drive and determination to set in motion something I really believed in. It was a renewed faith—in myself and my skills—based on what I'd learned, seen, thought, felt, heard, and understood. Life is the greatest teacher if we only take the time to open our minds and hearts and learn.

Abundance becomes success when you move from influencing others to influencing yourself. Your wonderful journey has begun.

I began writing my thoughts and feelings in this precious vessel (my diary/ journal) in 1988, prompted by the birth (an incredible gift) of my beautiful son Kayle. For the first time I had at my fingertips a place to securely record my dreams, emotions, thoughts, and visions. I refused to record any negative material because I believed it was counter-productive. Instead, I decided to write everything that was uplifting and colorful, warm and inviting. It represented the positive and enriching things driving me forward in spite of sometimes difficult circumstances. I wondered why I had not thought of it earlier. I obviously wasn't ready for that moment of profound awakening. It Became another amazing "aha" moment.

I was searching for answers to many questions and began using my journal as a precious record of all my quotations I had recovered from the various places I'd secreted them over the years (serendipity is an amazing thing). While looking for other things, I literally stumbled upon the many places I'd written those treasured writings from that very first time at my aunt's country home. I began adding to them as the flashes of energy and passion passed through my mind and my heart.

I continue the practice, and derive as much pleasure from it now as I did all those years ago. The quotations represent the creativity, color, drive, and enthusiasm in my life. They are the wonderfully empowering emotions driving me on a quest to embrace my purpose and find prosperity in my life.

I had been experimenting with the notion of writing and recording positive thoughts and affirmations in one key area for ready reference. It's something I still do every day. It serves to remind me of how rich and empowered my life truly is and how incredible our world can be if we simply have faith.

When you have inspiration driving every aspect of your life, you'll find it an absolute joy to motivate and empower others.

It hit me like a bolt of lightning on that magical day in July of 1988. Up until then, the idea of an uplifting and thought provoking personal journal was something I'd previously only briefly contemplated but never moved on for many reasons. I had given no thought to the value of such a fundamentally important resource. Apathy and an entire gauntlet of mixed emotions had, until that moment, totally overshadowed my life and prevented me from doing anything constructive.

Sure, I had used a journal for a number of years but only as a work tool. The idea of using one for empowerment purposes had not entered my mind. Until that time I had used note pads and scraps of paper to record my material. I hadn't really placed a great deal of importance on that process.

With the birth of my beautiful son Kayle (I actually delivered him), I suddenly realized there was more to my life than I was experiencing at that time. These feelings of deep love and affection accelerated the catalyst for change. I knew it was necessary. I could at last begin to "see" the endless possibilities unfolding in my increasingly unbelievable life. It was suddenly more meaningful. It became a huge moment of realization for me!

Any given day is made up of countless hours, minutes, seconds, emotions, dreams, plans, and thoughts of happiness, joy, love, gratitude, faith, optimism, drive, and success. Make every one count.

My journal was suddenly born as the one central (and very personal) place where I could record those feelings, emotions, images, thoughts, and notions pushing my life forward. This would have been a brilliant awakening all those years before if I had initiated it when I first began writing. It was a special place to record all those quotations I had scattered far and wide. It was a milestone—better late than never.

This became an extremely enlightening time for me as the importance of that moment began to dawn. It was a time of true enlightenment, and from that point my future became real and tangible.

For the first time I had a genuine anchor where every positive impact on my life could be instantly called upon to keep me focused, upbeat, and on track. It was literally akin to an epiphany.

The clouds suddenly parted and the sun began to shine in all aspects of my wonderful existence. I knew beyond question the road ahead would not always be smooth, but I was on the right path to a special form of empowerment. I was gaining control over my life and the direction I was heading. It was a truly magic moment—an exhilarating time in my life.

Your journal is also an ideal repository for your "to do" lists (see my previous book, *The Unstoppable Power Within*, Chapter 14: "The Value of Effective Time Management"), divided into short, medium, and long term goals. It allows you to keep abreast of your tasks and mark them off as you accomplish them. It becomes a great record of accomplishment.

Though it might take some time for things to improve, stay focused and maintain your journal to assist you to see the color and clarity in every moment. Unhitch yourself from your negative and uninspired life and refuse to accept anything not uplifting or positive.

> Peace and contentment are found when you have the courage to confront your problems, and show true gratitude for the subsequent victory over adversity.

Ensure your journal remains an honest and passionate record of your life's achievements. It will keep you on track during the times when doubt creeps into your routine. With renewed enthusiasm, the pain and anguish of setback will diminish as each day passes and moments of success and happiness fill your life.

In my journal I record such things as:

- Letter to my higher Self
- Letter to God (it need not be particularly religious—simply a letter of gratitude to the universal power existing for and in all of us)
- My hierarchy of values
- Personal inspirational quotations
- Mission statement
- Statement of purpose
- Goals
- Dreams
- Plans
- Targets
- Vision
- Personal wishes
- List of gratitudes (for all that's amazing in my life)
- A perfect day, every day
- My dedication and covenant

The journal is also a great filing system for information to assist the growth (and healing) process. It adds depth and direction to life. I combine this with visualization of those things I am grateful for right *now*. I make them real and tangible each morning and evening. I'm confident I won't ever arrive at a final destination (excluding the inevitability of death) as each day takes me to a great new place on my journey.

Always have gratitude for what you've achieved, for everyone you have met, and for those things teaching you important lessons. Doors will continue to open on opportunities at each turn as your days are filled with faith, respect, determination, and focus.

Ensure you record in your journal your many achievements, large and small, as a constant and lasting reminder of your true capabilities and a history of your wonderful and fulfilling journey to your destiny.

> With the right action, today is a brilliant rehearsal for the future. Use the time wisely and don't squander even one opportunity. It will lead to a brilliant finale.

When you make up your mind to incorporate your journal into everyday life, the list of possible topics is endless. Use headings that move you and makes your life inspired. This includes information about your ideal world and those things that continue to bring you endless happiness. It's those people, places, and moments offering positive thoughts and cherished memories, where you've laughed out loud and been unafraid to shed tears of joy. It's those times when you have been touched by memorable occasions and achieved great milestones; you've smiled and enjoyed happy and life-enriching incidents.

> The amount of wealth you create in your life will be directly proportionate to the power of the thought processes you dedicate to empowering your dreams and visions.

You can also include all your daily achievements for which you give thanks. Don't be afraid to add color and passion to what you include. It is, after all, a story of your life. It chronicles the many ways you're realizing your successes. It helps you maintain focus and passion and provides the positive reinforcement you'll undoubtedly need from time to time.

In addition to your many successes, ensure you record your positive thoughts, feelings, and emotions. Even small changes are integral to your wonderful journey. It remains a priceless record of your feelings and emotions throughout your brilliant voyage of discovery.

Your journal is an ideal place for all the information and emotions forming the basis of the incredible memories you will have in years to come. It is a priceless record of all your extraordinary triumphs over adversity throughout an astonishing life. It becomes a chronological record of your wonderful and empowering journey to abundance.

There's no hard and fast rule on the contents of your journal. It should be uplifting and moving, as a constant reminder of your incredible growth and development. Be proud of all your achievements; be exceedingly happy with the contents.

In your journal, as on your Creation Board, include photographs of yourself in joyous situations, surrounded by the people you love and the things you desire. Develop the ideal life by bringing the images, thoughts, words, and emotions into the here and now.

Stop procrastinating, step out of the shadows of mediocrity today, and begin living your ideal life.

Fill your journal with self-congratulatory messages (not arrogance or self-aggrandizement). Express your feelings confidently and display a high degree of self-respect and admiration for your achievements. Display a great deal of gratitude; it greatly elevates those feelings of self-worth.

The profound changes will become obvious in many aspects of your life. Even in those times when you feel less than magnificent, continue to hold yourself in high regard. Keep a powerful and lasting grasp on the positive energy in your journey.

The life you lead and the warmth and power radiating from you as a gracious, effervescent, and thankful human being is a true indication of your success. These wonderful traits act as a magnet for others seeking the light, power, confidence, and guidance you give freely.

Each time you congratulate yourself on a job well done, more opportunities will suddenly begin to manifest in your life.

Success happens regularly to people just like you and me. Happiness thrives in bright places. Develop your plan with affirmative action (nothing will happen without it), and begin the process of forward motion. Be encouraged as your vivid future begins to unfold. Maintain the right frame of mind, be passionate and enthusiastic, do your homework, and make decisions about and provisions for every conceivable contingency.

When periods of darkness and uncertainty threaten to overpower you, seek professional intervention to help lift you out of the depths. If you know someone in your life who is suffering, help them to find the assistance they need to improve their lives. Become a place of refuge and allow your inspired life to act as a beacon of hope for others. Like you, they too deserve to be happy.

Trust your heart and be encouraged by your dreams. All this greatness should be recorded in your journal so in ten, twenty, and even thirty years, you can look back at your wonderful life and even pass it on to your children or those under your care and guidance as a record of success over adversity and a priceless and indispensable mentoring tool.

My life is teeming with endless possibilities, and success comes from my ability to capitalize on every opportunity arising in my world.

LESSONS LEARNED

1. Your journal is a precious record of your positive thoughts, words, actions, and achievements.

2. Fill the pages of your journal with joyful and uplifting moments.

3. Always have gratitude for what you achieve.

4. Congratulate yourself for your milestones.

5. Include in your journal all information about the positive aspects of your ideal life.

6. Your diary/journal is an ideal storehouse for your "to do" lists.

7. Record your admiration and respect for yourself and your incredible world.

8. Allow your self-worth and high self-regard to shine.

9. Success happens every day to people just like you and me.

10. Use your journal as a record of achievement for the benefit of yourself and others.

Chapter 6

THE MAINTENANCE OF YOUR SELF-ESTEEM

Every day of our lives, each of us is presented with
new opportunities to interact with others in positive
and uplifting ways. Don't waste the chance to make
a real and impacting difference in their lives.

❧

Throughout my early development, I constantly suffered from low self-esteem. Through my years of stuttering and the ensuing bullying, I found no solace in any aspect of my life. I was in tears most nights as I cried myself to sleep. I just wanted it to stop, but somehow I knew it wouldn't. I have no doubt many readers have found themselves in this very same position. It's becomes a very lonely and isolated place to be.

There were some bright moments with family members and a few close friends. However, I struggled every day with self-image issues and my feelings of self-worth were at an all-time low. I didn't feel there was anything left for me. Life was dark and the view of the future became almost ompletely obscured by negativity.

I learned many lessons during this time of uncertainty. It was a struggle to remain focused, but somewhere inside I knew things would get better. At least I hoped they would, and I kept my faith in that notion. It became a very powerful anchor for me. Surely the pall of darkness couldn't remain over my life forever.

It is important to maintain your spirit. Care for yourself, inside and out. Support and nourish all aspects of your life. Don't wait until you hit rock bottom before you seek assistance. I never looked for any kind of support and suffered in silence. It took ten years before I was able to unshackle myself and walk out into the bright light of effective communication. I consider myself fortunate.

Don't allow that to happen to you or others in your life. Take positive, life-enriching action to stop the pain. If necessary, speak to family members and friends. Likewise, if you see someone in your life who is suffering, speak up and reach out. Become the help a person might need to empower and enrich their life.

There can be no question—high self-esteem is fundamental to your growth and development. Always have a love and respect for yourself and your ability. If you don't like and believe in the person you are with a total regard for every aspect of your life, then I guarantee success and abundance will elude you. You can't hope to attract great things into your sphere if you lack confidence, faith, love, and gratitude in every aspect of your existence.

> Accomplishment is found in one's capacity to rise to any occasion and systematically overcome the challenges encountered.

Begin the process of building your self-esteem by systematically creating and nurturing a Self in and with whom you are comfortable—a wonderfully balanced, loving, and happy individual whom you like, love, respect, and understand. You are after all a tremendously gifted, creative, and capable individual in whom you wholeheartedly believe. Embrace your ability to impact positively on others every day in countless ways.

Like any functional tool for personal development, your self-esteem requires ongoing maintenance. Once you build it, you have to constantly work to keep it high, strong, and relevant. *You* must consistently nurture and support it. First and foremost, develop a belief in yourself and all you're capable of achieving. Understand the impact your words and actions have on others.

There will always be people on the peripheral of your life who won't support, encourage, congratulate, or acknowledge you, no matter how successful you strive to be. This negative energy is based on that other person's jealousy of what you have in your life and the principles supporting every aspect of your world. The void grows exponentially as they see you accelerating your life and living a full and empowered existence as they continue to wallow in a sea of self-pity and under-achievement.

Don't waste time trying to bridge this gap. Move forward with optimism, enthusiasm, and gratitude as you continue to grow and prosper. Many people will invariably follow you—others will not. Continue to forge a path, first for yourself and then for those with the vision and confidence to follow you, irrespective of the opposition you face.

"From today on I will not allow others to steal my dreams, negatively impact my self-esteem or confidence, or derail me from my purpose. I'm strong, positive, and determined. Success is my goal."

When your thoughts, words, and actions come from a positive place, those few negative individuals who try to impede your progress will no longer impact you. Be influenced instead by the positive contact you have with the majority and how they react to you. Allow the wonderfully warm interaction you enjoy with them on a daily basis to empower your journey.

The life we lead and the effect others might have on our existence will have a profound influence on the way we look at ourselves and how we feel about our "inner being." Many of us have a mask we put in a box beside the door and only wear it when we leave the house or interact with others. We use it as a protection mechanism to cover our low self-esteem and lack of self-confidence. This fragile cover we adopt can't last. Sooner or later the façade breaks down and the true self is revealed.

This is not an incurable disease. It's not an injury or irreversible procedure. While it can impact us in a negative way, it's a transitory state of being—a temporary state of mind. We need to enrich our lives and permit ourselves to be the best we can.

> Once you find and accentuate your posture, improved self-esteem will follow.

There are several steps you can take each and every day to improve your life, to liven yourself up if you suffer from low self-esteem:

- *Set clear goals* before you embark on any interaction. Write them down and know exactly what aspect of your life you wish to alter.

- *Make one change at a time* so you won't become disheartened with temporary setbacks.

- *Understand how each interaction* you have can assist (has assisted) your growth and development.

- *Improve your posture with a smile*, firm handshake, and eye contact. While it might initially seem a struggle which can take you right out of your comfort zone, each interaction will begin to build your confidence.

- *Practice affirmative (open) body language* and you'll notice changes occurring almost immediately as others warm to your friendly approach and engaging nature.

- *Develop your communication skills* through listening and remembering names, dates, places, and conversations. Don't be afraid to ask a person's name a second time and recheck details to ensure you have the correct information. Always stay with the conversation, contribute where appropriate, and allow the other person to express a confident point of view.

- *Pay attention to others and make them feel important.* This will have a mirror effect as others respond to your optimistic approach.

- *Be happy and always willing to congratulate yourself.* This will keep your spirits high.

- *Accept praise from others with gratitude.* Other people will want to thank you for your support and encouragement. Freely accept it with humility.

While the above is by no means an exhaustive list of affirmative steps, constant practice develops your self-esteem. As you grow, people will be attracted to you, and once you master the steps you'll notice marked changes in your career and personal life. Your positive interaction with others and the way you feel about yourself ultimately determines the power and longevity of your self-esteem. You grow in confidence as these positive feelings are reciprocated.

> To have others believe in me has some importance in shaping my life. However, what I believe of myself is paramount to my good health, happiness, success, and development.

Individuals possessed of high self-esteem tend to view life and circumstances in a positive light. They appear to perform better in the work environment and, on the whole, have less to complain about. They certainly appear more confident in all aspects of their daily lives, generally remaining unscathed by the negative comments of others.

High self-esteem is crucial to the ongoing positive development of our personal and professional lives. It can't be found in a book or a bottle and is definitely not a form of magic. It can neither be bought nor borrowed. It will certainly not be mystically manifested.

With external pressure exerted on us through the criticism of others, we can lose our way and feel the crushing effects of our momentary inability to rise above adversity. We can tend to retreat into ourselves as a protection mechanism, and as a consequence our self-esteem weakens and feelings of self-worth greatly diminish. Each of us holds in our hands the key to life's amazing treasures when we learn to be in touch with our true Self.

> Warmly embrace the power of the three "selves" in your life—self-belief, self-esteem, and self-worth. Hold them firmly in your heart and your hands and you'll be unstoppable.

Meet, greet, accept, respect, and embrace your inner self; believe you are a wonderful and worthy person in spite of what others might say or do to affect you. They cannot influence you unless you let down your guard and allow them entry to your feelings and emotions locker. Learn to take control of your life. Begin to live it to the full.

The top 2 percent of achievers in the world understands the value of self-empowerment. They don't allow others to unfavorably affect their judgment or progress. These are the very same people who control much of the wealth. They understand the intrinsic nature of success and abundance and have at their disposal the tools necessary to achieve unimaginable prosperity.

These very focused and driven individuals can constantly remain successful, with a total and unqualified belief in their own abilities, because they know who they are. They understand absolutely how much their lives are worth. They hold a very conscious regard for the power and importance of the paths they follow and the quality in the future unfolding before them.

These are the same people who can rise like a phoenix from the ashes of ruin and even surpass their previous levels of wealth and prosperity. They hold fast to this unfailing belief in their power to achieve in spite of the crushing obstacles they face.

> To be an incredible success in all aspects of your life, you must first believe yourself worthy and then learn to accelerate the opportunities flooding into your world.

Those, on the other hand, who labor under the devastating prison of low self-esteem and unproductive feelings of low self-worth generally have a dislike of their lives and circumstances. Much of what they do and the way they view life constantly spirals out of control as they continue the downward slide in most aspects of their existence. Very little of what they do, say, feel, or experience in their daily lives has a positive impact their futures. They have problems assimilating and rarely enjoy the company of positive and driven people.

These individuals often believe they're viewed as demotivated and rudderless by the individuals who are focused and passionate about their lives. They have some difficulty connecting with others, particularly those who are successful.

These disenchanted people need only open their eyes and their hearts and believe in themselves. They begin creating the ideal life through supporting and understanding their own true selves. It's important for them to instigate a strict regimen of support for their highest values and believe in the relevance and importance of the lives they lead.

If they are leading unproductive lives they can only change if they realize the futility of their current position and take appropriate action to change it. Intervention is often required to assist these individuals in getting their lives back on track.

> Self-esteem is like any incredible construction. If you take your time and build it piece by piece on a sound foundation, it will become an amazingly powerful and reliable asset to you every day.

Low self-esteem generally results in under-performance in the workplace and a failure to present well under pressure. These unfortunate individuals are more often affected by the negative comments of others. It becomes self-perpetuating when there appears no way out as the clouds of despair become all-encompassing.

Self-esteem and self-worth are linked, although they are not one and the same. Self-esteem is often driven by the impact of the words and actions of others. High self-esteem can help us feel good about ourselves and affect the confidence and pride we have in our personal appearance. It can also impact the success we enjoy through the level of performance in the job we do. This can change depending upon the circumstances in which we find ourselves at any given time. We may be very confident in what we do and the life we lead. However, when in an unfamiliar or challenging situation, such as standing on the podium or working in a totally unfamiliar environment, we might feel less than we should and suffer some form of nerves. At that point, our confidence could suffer and feelings of self-worth diminish.

When people pat us on the back or give us accolades because we've done a great job, it serves to escalate the positive feelings we hold about ourselves in relation to the specific task or action. In those instances, it serves to raise our self-esteem. It's also driven by the reactions of others to us in terms of our standing in the community—our words and actions—and the impact we have on the world around us.

> You create your own reality every day of your life. Ensure you base it on your own dreams and visions and your self-worth—never as the result of the image dictated by others.

Self-worth, on the other hand, is the value we put on our life and the way we live it—a measure of the respect we have for ourselves according to our actions and interactions. Are you deserving of good things in your life? Are you a nice person? Do you enjoy sound relationships with family members, business associates, friends, and neighbors? Are you generous, supportive, encouraging, loving, and caring?

Many of us mistakenly believe that self-worth is measured in terms of our personal wealth. In actual fact, we may for all intents and purposes be virtually penniless and still have a very high degree of self-worth. We may be good entrepreneurs, parents, siblings, partners, or neighbors and happy in our assistance to and interactions with others. It's measured by the value we put on ourselves, our lives, and the contributions we make to society—the measure of the person we are and believe ourselves to be. This can, of course, be affected by our self-esteem.

If you have a high regard for yourself and your ability, then your feelings of your own worth will be elevated. On the contrary, if you don't hold yourself and your ability in high regard, it stands to reason your self-worth will be at very low ebb. It's here you need to consider how you can fix this problem.

> When you waste time searching for acceptance in the eyes of others, you won't see and appreciate yourself in a fresh, positive, and compassionate light.

Every dream you experience, thought you have, and vision you hold about yourself and your future will begin the process of creating a significant self-regard. It's a monumental journey to the point where you respect your inner self, simply because you're a nice person and strive for good in your own life and in the lives of others. This will give you self-love in abundance and be reflected in the words and actions of others.

Highs and lows occur at every turn in our lives. As we ride the ebb and flow of the journey we undertake, we learn that various aspects of our environment and our reactions will have a profound effect on the way we feel about ourselves. It's called human nature and is at the core of our very being. Our reaction to these influences can determine the success or otherwise of our lives. It's not always an easy trip we take, especially if we begin at a very low point in our lives.

Our future is so often impacted by those who come into and out of our personal space and is determined largely by how we interact with these individuals and react to various stimuli in our daily lives. It's also a result of our response to how others claim to see us and what is said about us, both to our faces and behind our backs.

We're human, with all the emotions and feelings that accompany that, and therefore won't feel good about ourselves every moment of the day. Nor will we always hold ourselves in high regard or feel the value of our worth.

To believe otherwise would be foolish and quite simply a deception. The real answer is to rise above the negativity of others (and our own)—not always easy, but with practice and professional assistance where necessary, it can be successfully achieved.

> When you believe there's nothing but limitation and failure in your life, you've already embraced it.

Many people are adept at transferring their negativity to others in a vain and totally misguided attempt to remain guilt-free and build some type of disjointed self-regard. By this action, they live under the misapprehension that they somehow absolve themselves of their obligation to act with common decency and respect toward others.

In effect, they endeavor to transfer those often overwhelming feelings of inadequacy they hold about themselves and their lives. It's used as a coping mechanism so they don't have to confront the darkness of their own shallow existences and deal with their own inadequacies.

Deep down, these individuals know they are living a lie and at some subconscious level understand what they are doing is wrong. Many do not have the courage and discipline to stop this detrimental and potentially destructive behavior and, as a consequence, it becomes the norm.

> Those who tell you that you can't surely know in their own hearts they never will.

Ignore the negativity of others and their adverse actions. Ensure those barbs remain in the wilderness where they belong. Learn to release your troubles and don't add to them by taking on board the baggage willingly imparted by others. Put the negativity in the bin where it belongs and make space for the exciting things beginning to fill all corners of your world. Look for the light rather than dwelling on the darkness and learn to protect yourself from pessimism.

Continue to congratulate yourself for things well done, reward yourself for successes, and learn from the lessons life brings to your door. You will be well on your way to building your self-esteem and self-worth.

While others are stumbling in the darkness of their own making, you can choose to flourish. You feed your positive and driven emotions with the burst of power and energy you create in your determination to refuse to accept the negativity of those who continue to punish themselves. These people can so easily pull you into the mire if you don't allow the fuel of your focus and resolve to turn their negative energy into positive motion.

I can't stress enough the need to seek professional assistance when you feel the walls of gloominess closing in on your life. There's no shame in asking for help. Sometimes it's difficult for us to see when life is closing in on us, and so it's up to others to look out for our welfare.

Seek from others the positive input you need to get your life back on track and begin the process of rebuilding your self-esteem and recovering your feelings of self-worth.

Always keep your head high, even in the face of monumental struggle. Bad weather will eventually pass and calm seas return once more. That's your time to shine.

LESSONS LEARNED

1. High self-esteem is fundamental to growth and development.

2. Believe in yourself and you will attract good things into your life.

3. Self-esteem and self-worth are linked.

4. Each day, every aspect of our behavior impacts our self-regard.

5. There are several steps to assist in developing and supporting your self-esteem:

   - Set clear goals. Write them down before you begin to interact.

   - Make one change at a time and check your progress.

   - Understand how each interaction can assist (has assisted) your growth and development.

   - Improve your posture with a smile, firm handshake, and eye contact.

   - Practice affirmative (open) body language.

   - Develop your communication skills. Listen and remember names, dates, places, and conversations.

   - Pay attention to others and make them feel important.

   - Be happy and always willing to congratulate yourself.

6. Many of us wear a mask to hide the "inner self."

7. Low self-esteem is not incurable or irreversible.

8. The level of our self-esteem is a result of interactions in our lives.

9. Rising above negativity is a real step in building self-esteem.

10. Never allow others to impact negatively on your life.

11. Don't carry your troubles around. Release them and look to a great future.

12. Always congratulate and reward yourself for achievements.

13. Feed on the negativity of others—make it a positive, focused, and determined force.

14. Look to family and friends for support when necessary.

15. Never be afraid or ashamed to seek professional assistance.

Chapter 7

EMBRACE WHAT SUCCESS CAN DELIVER

When you choose to sit at the back of the aircraft on
your journey through life, you will continue to miss the
fantastic view that constantly unfolds before you

The American industrialist and philanthropist John Davison Rockefeller saw
genuine affluence during the Great Depression, where others found despair.
He famously proclaimed, "If you want to succeed, you should strike out on
new paths rather than travel the worn paths of accepted success."[1]

How many of us have literally had success in our hands and watched it
simply vanish? Whether on a personal level, in a business enterprise, or on the
sporting field, it can so easily fall from our grasp and leave us feeling totally
deflated. It has certainly happened to me on more than one occasion.

The list of fears and phobias haunting so many of us is almost endless. It
includes death, poverty, loneliness, spiders, failure, ridicule, flying, rejection,
heights, the dark, water, and speaking in public. There is also a fear of success.
"What will we do once we get there (wherever *there* is)?" "If we don't focus our
full attention on that special place, will we ever arrive?" "Will I know when
I get there?" "How will I possibly stay focused and on top of things?" "What

will I do with the responsibility I have?" Of course, there's the age-old argument: "Things are pretty good the way they are. Why should I rock the boat?"

Once you make up your mind to succeed, failure is never an option.

More often than not, it's the emotional rollercoaster ride associated with fear rather than the fear itself that affects us and determines the responses we have to the various stimuli. We must find the courage within to face those fears and overcome them.

Success is a state of being where we enjoy the fruits of our labor. It becomes an all-embracing situation with incredible opportunities to continually realize our dreams and goals.

This special place invites feelings of elation. It becomes an incredible position of quiet understanding with the knowledge that you've done your best with your life and are continuing on that journey to realize everything you desire. It also represents a strong focus, where you know beyond question you are on track and traveling in the right direction. It's beyond wondering about "what might be" and rather embracing "what is" and "what's awaiting me on the horizon."

To seek a better life is never about the possibility of rocking the boat. The fact you're looking for assistance means things are not as good as you might wish to convince yourself they are. No matter how bad you think things might be, with some effort, focus, and a committed plan of action, aspects of life can and will improve.

Most people fail not because they don't embrace success, but rather because they most fear it and the responsibilities it brings.

This is the time to get out of your lethargy, pull yourself out of the armchair of apathy, and grasp every opportunity as it passes through your life. Feeling sorry for yourself and your situation won't improve anything. Pretending your life is fine as it is will also not make things better. Having a lackluster attitude will only ensure you remain locked in your prison of mediocrity.

Success is never your enemy. *Hesitation* is. *Apathy* is. *Fear* is. *Procrastination* is and *failure* certainly is. We all too often willingly embrace one or more of these traits without knowing or acknowledging the impact they do (and will) have on our welfare, our future, and the ability to embrace abundance in our lives. They often represent the paths of least resistance in life, and we embrace them without thinking of the possible or probable consequences.

Quite often we hesitate simply because we're afraid of the (assumed) enormity of the task ahead, or we lack confidence in ourselves and our abilities. Procrastination is a high, wide, and often impenetrable wall we build to protect ourselves from some eventual outcome we fear (often without justification).

Far too often we dither and postpone many tasks because we see the overall job as just too big to handle, too overwhelming, or we simply lack the courage and wherewithal to take that step out of our comfort zones. The journey is only ever as daunting as we decide it is. The future—whatever we want it to be—is squarely in our own hands.

The secret to completing the tasks required in our lives is to divide them up and do one at a time. If you do each task as a separate entity, it will make the overall job that much smaller and easier to manage. It can eliminate the fear of a huge, looming force you have to work against. This enables you to see and fully appreciate the advancements you make.

> Once you begin to understand, appreciate, and embrace the world around you—with all its fault and problems—you'll begin to receive the goodness and success accompanying it.

Check off each task as you complete it. This will boost your confidence and allow you to see your goals so much clearer, make them less overwhelming and, therefore, increasingly more attainable.

When you engage a very positive frame of mind, the forward momentum, energy, and excitement will carry you in the direction you wish to go. You gather speed as you move ahead, and with this increase in pace comes a confidence boost. Excitement and energy build as you see and celebrate your daily accomplishments.

When you systematically complete each task, the overall mission becomes far less foreboding. Your confidence grows as you continue on this wonderful journey. It gives you the drive and enthusiasm to continue.

Don't waste time concentrating on what might have had a negative impact on your life or focus any attention on the incorrect choices you've made. Always—and I mean *always*—focus your attention on what you do right—on what's working and what brings you joy and happiness.

It's okay to give fleeting thought to what didn't go well; it serves to keep you on track for a stellar future and allows you to make appropriate changes to your plan. Never spend too much time dwelling in the past; leave it where it belongs. Look to the future with great optimism and enthusiasm.

The view to the front, no matter how small it might initially appear, is always clearer, brighter, and more enticing than it is from the rear. If you concentrate too much on where you've been, you won't have the time, energy, or focus to see where you're going and fully embrace the opportunities as they arise. Each time you look over your shoulder at the past, you run the very real risk of missing great opportunities in the present.

> No one has ever achieved truly great things with an attitude of failure and defeat. Belief and a strong plan of action open some wonderful doors to your incredible future.

It is possible to set yourself up for incredible success and abundance with the right tools and positive state of mind. Of course, it generally doesn't come easily. The measure of who you are and who you are ultimately to become is determined by the choices you make and the courage you show when you confront barriers. We all have the power of (forward) vision; we need only tap in and learn to use this incredible resource to our advantage.

No doubt you've heard of many of the following people: Bill Gates, Warren Buffet, Ted Turner, Donald Trump, Ralph Lauren, Oprah Winfrey, Steven Spielberg, Sir Richard Branson, Dennis Tito, Michael Dell, Larry Ellison, Mark Zuckerberg, Jack Dorsey, and Rupert Murdoch. If not all then certainly some of these names should be familiar to you.

Having risen to positions of authority and great responsibility within their chosen fields, these achievers, along with countless others who strive for greatness in their lives, possess a unique perception of the social conscience accompanying their situation. Wealth and abundance carry this legacy and are inescapably linked to the power of responsibility.

> To be happy and successful, you don't necessarily have to have the best of everything. You simply need the mindset to make the best of everything.

Fear of success often indicates a fear of responsibility. Success and abundance bring with them a duty to assist those who are less fortunate than we who have affluence in our lives. Charity begins at home, but it really can't be allowed to remain there because it will stagnate.

I'm convinced that an individual will never rise to a position of incredible success and abundance in life without a strong and inherent belief in the power of assistance to others. When you have success and abundance in your life, others will place expectations on you, your time, and your assets, because success brings with it a degree of social responsibility. When you have abundance, you have a duty to assist those who do not. How you choose to exercise that responsibility is entirely up to you.

It could take the form of certain social welfare programs, setting up charitable institutions of your own (there are strict guidelines in place in most countries to monitor and regulate the establishment of charities, to eliminate the possibility of fraud), or simply doing good turns with your time, skills, and, in some cases, money.

> Failure, like weeds, flourishes in the darkness. Always fill your life with light, color, and faith.

Don't be afraid of failure. While you only allow it to be a temporary measure, it develops in you the intestinal fortitude to look at yourself and your journey and determine the changes you need to make in order to put your life back on track. Failure is not one constant; it's a succession of wrong steps you initially fail to recognize and change. Once you accept them as norms in your life, you've already embraced disappointment and negativity.

Life puts hurdles in our way to make us stop, look, listen, and change. If we continue to make the same error, it becomes a mistake. It's important to stop, examine our actions, and make appropriate changes. Embrace change and signal our intention to move forward. In doing this we put our lives back on track.

A constant fear of under-achievement at the forefront of your mind ultimately invites failure to become a solid part of your psyche. Procrastination in respect to your goals and dreams will see your life consistently beset by problems. When you embrace an all-pervading and systematic belief in those doubts through constant feeding, it becomes a solid component of your psyche.

In this very lonely place, you waste precious time and effort on these self-perpetuating and destructive negative emotions. They can so easily take you into the darkness of failure and misery.

> With the right action, today is a brilliant rehearsal for the future. Use the time wisely, and don't squander even one opportunity. It will lead to a brilliant finale.

Fully embrace the notion of success as it comes into your world each and every day. Open the doors and windows to invite it to flow through every aspect of your existence. When you can do this without procrastination or fear, you begin to understand how it feels to open your mind to positive thinking. Invite success and prosperity to be a full and functional part of your wonderful life.

This frame of mind in a complete form assists you to move beyond simply wishing and hoping into the realm of absolute knowing. Firmly establish this state of mind as a functional part of your life, and you won't waste precious time thinking about failure on the occasions it passes your door.

With an unwavering belief in your own power as a success magnet, you give little or no thought to any disappointment in your life. You always have the absolute mindset of prosperity in spite of what you may encounter that could otherwise have the capacity to push you from your forward journey.

There will be times when you stand on the threshold, deciding whether or not to answer the door. If you do and you hold fast to your beliefs and determination, you will have the positive attitude necessary to shrug off any future possibility of failure.

A positive state of mind attracts even greater phenomena into your life. It will also develop in you the resolve to deal positively with obstacles as they arise. You will be more able to seek and find plausible solutions and apply the required focus and determination to achieve your goals.

The realms of possibility that exist within each of us are largely unfathomable.

Remez Sasson, the prolific self-improvement author, takes an enamored stance on positive thinking. He wrote the words, "Change the mental movie that you keep viewing in your mind to one that you like. Keep playing it in your mind, and before you know it, the movie turns into reality."[2]

Embrace success and make it a part of your everyday psyche. Never underestimate yourself, your plan of action, dreams, determination, or the length, depth, *and* excitement of the journey you're taking.

If something isn't working, change it. If an obstacle won't move or dissolve and you can't go through it, find a way around it. Keep the faith and continue to move in a forward direction.

Never become anxious or disillusioned when the going gets a little tough. It will happen many times on your journey. Remember why you're working as passionately and as hard as you are.

Likewise, never shy away from or be afraid of success. It comes in many forms and will add a profound depth, color, and meaning to your life and the lives of those you touch. It also brings with it real responsibilities. Your newfound strength and confidence will also bring you the passion and focus to deal with the many and varied challenges of success and the very real ability and self-reliance to deal thoughtfully and honestly with them.

Toughen up, push up your sleeves, and roll with the punches. Decide to be in the rainbow for the long haul in spite of what you might encounter and regardless of how tough your travels might become. It's a much richer and more rewarding place than the alternative.

Embrace the responsibility of success. It brings you a new understanding of compassion and gratitude and opens the doors to even greater rewards.

Be openly accepting of the responsibilities, to yourself and others, brought by success. Understand and recognize the ramifications, for in that realm you are adding depth and substance to your spiritual self and profoundly aiding your growth and development on a number of critical levels. It's a richly rewarding journey.

Be confident when you ask for assistance from those with experience. Share your journey with family members and friends and savor the many incredible achievements along the way. Never be deterred by the negativity of others, and in spite of the barbs of those detractors keep your composure, remain focused, and stay with the journey.

Your future is unfolding right now and will continue to do so irrespective of the action you take. With belief and steely determination, success will manifest in your life in the way you envisage when you find the faith and courage to remain focused and build the future you want.

NOTES

1. John D. Rockefeller , qtd. in Zig Ziglar, *Steps to the Top* (Gretna: Pelican Pub., 1985), 16.

2. Remez Sasson, "Quotes on Success and on Attaining Success," Success Quotes, accessed February 18, 2015, http://www.successconsciousness.com/index_000018.htm.

When I bring into my life the ability to successfully eliminate negative thoughts, words, and actions, I begin the fulfilling process of building a strong and supported platform of positive growth and development. This is the foundation of my success and abundance.

LESSONS LEARNED

1. Fear of success is often a fear of the responsibility it brings.

2. Self-pity will always anchor you to your problems.

3. Success by its very nature can in no way be your enemy.

4. Always focus on what brings you joy and happiness.

5. Success will continue to open some wonderful doors in your life.

6. Once you embrace positive change, you put your life back on track.

7. Always commit to a belief in the power and goodness of assistance to others.

8. Learn to embrace success and invite it into your life.

9. Be openly accepting of responsibility to yourself and others.

10. In accepting responsibility, you add depth and substance to your existence.

11. Openly encourage success into your life, and you won't be fazed by hurdles.

12. Never underestimate yourself, your plan of action, or the journey you're taking.

13. Don't be afraid to ask for assistance from those with experience.

14. Share your journey with family members and friends and savor all experiences.

Chapter 8

KEEP YOUR MIND, ENERGY, AND FOCUS ON THE PRIZE

Like a great doctor, you should learn to scrutinize your own life. If it's ailing, examine the symptoms and work effectively to eliminate the cause. Ensure it leads to a wonderful and empowered future.

What if you were told by "a friend" that you were considered over the hill at 38 years of age and that your life would never amount to anything? What if that person said that all life's opportunities had passed you by? How would you feel? Would you be crestfallen? Would it sadden you? More importantly, would it stop you from achieving your dreams and goals and fulfilling your purpose?

That's exactly what happened to me. I was 38 years of age and someone told me that my life would amount to nothing. I was too old to realize any degree of success in my life and I should stop daydreaming and begin living in reality. It was really offensive, and it hurt me deeply for a short time. This person had been a part of my life and just walked away. For a brief time I took the comments to heart. Then I recognized the nugget in those harsh words. I got back up and kept moving forward with an even greater resolve.

For those who don't know, daydreaming is a very real part of living in the present. It has been and continues to be a very real part of my journey. It helps us create the kind of life we really want. It keeps us focused and on target. Without those dreams, we have no image of the life we desire and, therefore, nothing concrete on which to build.

Given the often overwhelming nature of the world we live in and the constant hustle and bustle of everyday life, it's easy to allow our focus to wander from our goals. The dominant state of mind at any given time makes it also tempting to look over our shoulders at what has gone before. We can take our focus off the prize. It's so easy to do and happens quite often.

When this occurs, recognize it as a negative action and immediately rectify the situation so you remain on target. Bring your focus back to the road ahead.

Other people can also conspire to derail you from your plan. If you allow the negativity of outside influences to affect you, then it stands to reason you run the risk of losing the inspiration. Others are prone to react with potentially damaging responses through their jealousy and feelings of inadequacy at what they perceive as your drive and commitment to fully embrace success in your life.

When you give others the chance to adversely impact your self-esteem and feelings of self-worth, the brunt of their uninvited intervention could stall your drive and render your thoughts, actions, and efforts seemingly futile.

> Positive action and the associated success is simply the fundamental realization of our own capacity to achieve.

These are very often people in your circle—friends and confidantes— who have their own agendas to divert you from your path. Sometimes it's done with good intentions at what they believe are your misdirected energies (you are moving in a direction where they would never have the courage or vision to go). At other times their actions are driven by simple envy. Avoid them where possible and never discuss your plans with these people.

Always keep the prize in sight, irrespective of the challenges faced. Constantly review your plan, look at your Creation Board (see Chapter 4), and read your journal often (see Chapter 5). This will assist you to remain firmly on track and remind you of where you're going and the reason you are traveling this particular path—to embrace and build upon a secure, bright, happy, healthy, and abundant future.

Success is not one isolated event. Achievement never comes down to one race, business deal, project, or target. When you speak of success, you never mean in one particular moment in time or in one isolated aspect of your life.

It's a lifetime journey where moments of wonder and fulfillment, positive thought and action, even obstacles and troubles add up to a generation of triumphs. Remain on track and work consistently and diligently toward your incredible goals.

> The difference between successful people and those who are forever chasing that elusive prize is the determination, passion, drive, and commitment they display because they understand success and all it implies.

Keep your mind, energy, and total focus on the prize (your future) otherwise the view ahead will become distant and obscured to a point where you will be unable to see it. Your drive and passion will diminish, and you'll lose contact with the reason why you're following the path you're on. You will become sidetracked, and if you fail to regain the focus and passion I guarantee you will lose your commitment altogether.

Your future will become a very disjointed and vague destination no longer visible or attractive to you. It will be totally obscured by negative thoughts, emotions, distractions, and overwhelming feelings of failure and disenchantment. It will no longer have any real purpose in your life.

When clouds descend and you succumb to negative influences, mediocrity and deflation follow. In this state you believe opportunities have passed you by and those who sought to bring you down to their level were in fact right. Now you have become ordinary in your decision to relegate yourself to a life of mundane actions instead of extraordinary achievements.

If this is the kind of life you want, then do nothing and you will do everything to realize a future offering no real promise for success and abundance. Each day will blur into the next; there will be very little color and clarity in your destiny. You will have no stars to reach for and no rewards to reap along your journey.

> The measure of my success directly parallels my commitment to those around me and my determination to overcome the challenges I face each and every day.

When the past, the present, and the future become a blurred reality of monotonous inaction, your life will become a faded black and white sketch. However, your journey will be re-invigorated by warm colors and vibrant energy as you get back on track and regain your drive and commitment.

Whatever you truly and intensely believe will become your reality. Successful people have a firm and unwavering belief in themselves and a dogged determination to achieve their goals. They refuse to entertain any possibility that failure is an option.

Successful thinking is an unfaltering routine rather than a fleeting thought. It must fill the senses and be the foundation stone of your reality. Your thoughts and actions must be in total harmony with your beliefs. It becomes a centerpiece of your mental drive as you constantly strive ever closer to the big picture of your success.

Those who understand and embrace success in their lives recognize that problems do occur from time to time. It's in these moments those with an unrelenting confidence in themselves and their abilities hold on to their values with an avid determination.

Belief in yourself and your journey renders failure a momentary glitch. It becomes just another small obstacle in life. There might be many failures along the road; however, when you focus on the prize and the solution rather than the problem and you formulate appropriate and workable strategies to overcome adversity, your self-belief will continue to flourish and you'll keep moving forward.

> The degree of love and respect you have for yourself is determined by the fundamental investment you make in your life, future, and integrity. Make every thought, emotion, word, and action count for something truly special.

Create and live your own reality. It makes you less dependent on assistance from others. Discover greater confidence, courage, and depth within. Grow and flourish and don't rely solely on mentors for support and guidance. Find the courage and strength to stand on your own two feet. You'll begin to prosper as a truly successful person in your own right.

Mentors will be in your life for the long haul, but as time passes and you discover the strength you have to navigate your own life, they will have far less influence. They will be available for input and guidance at specific points on your journey.

Always act in total harmony with your innate beliefs. Remain focused on an absolutely successful outcome with unqualified conviction in the certainty of the road you're traveling. You will move from *believing you might* to *knowing you* can. There will be no doubt that your journey is taking you in the right direction and you're on the road to achieving success and abundance. It's an incredibly exhilarating place to be.

> Continue to create your own reality so you are never shackled by the fruits of another's success.

We all feel worn out and a little deflated from time to time. Its human nature. It's perfectly normal to feel down and frustrated on occasions, as long as it is only a temporary state of being. If it persists, take steps to regain your drive, passion, and focus. Seek professional help or intervention if necessary.

There will be those times in your life when you just want to close the curtains and curl up on the couch in your pajamas. It's imperative you try and shake yourself out of this lethargy. It can happen at any time. When you're between jobs—perhaps you've been laid off and begin to feel that things are hopeless. Maybe you confront obstacles, and at face value they appear insurmountable. It happens to us all from time to time when we just want to hide away and close out those things which adversely impact our lives.

For your own wellbeing, take whatever positive steps are necessary to remain connected to reality. Ignoring things won't make them go away. Problems won't just evaporate and challenges fade. While things might look better in the bright light of the new day, you have to really take control to get on top of issues.

There are some things you can do to lift the mood and bring some energy and color into your life. Ensure you rise of a morning at the time you would if you were going to work. You have to shower and run a comb through your hair. If you're a guy, have a shave if that's what you normally do, get dressed, and feel engaged with life. This is a signal to the universe that you're ready and willing to be a part of the world at large. It makes the positive connection that you are sincere about life and will allow nothing to stand in your way.

If you sit around and stay disconnected, you will begin to brood. It will soon become a part of your existence as your mind latches on to and identifies with the negative energy beginning to infiltrate all aspects of your life. Nip it squarely in the bud. Don't sit around in your pajamas brooding. Put on some good clothes and set about building a new life. Remain focused and positive, energetic, optimistic, and determined.

Ensure these instances are only momentary stops on your journey. Look for professional support and assistance if necessary to get you back on the right path and rebuild your self-belief and confidence. They are there waiting to again be an integral part of your existence, though just out of reach in those moments of fleeting darkness.

To enjoy the highs offered by life, you must also understand the necessity for lows.

LESSONS LEARNED

1. It is easy to allow our minds to wander from the view ahead.

2. Beware of those who will try and derail you.

3. Success is not one isolated event in life.

4. Work hard to bring about all you want in life.

5. Success is a lifetime journey.

6. Never allow yourself to become mediocre and ordinary.

7. Doing nothing is doing everything to realize an empty future.

8. Feeling down and deflated is normal as long as it's temporary.

9. Look for help and guidance when things get on top of you.

10. If the track remains sound, you can never be permanently derailed.

Chapter 9

THE IMPORTANCE OF POSITIVE CHANGE IN YOUR LIFE

The instant you commit to positive change in your life,
you begin to evolve into the person you envisage yourself
becoming. Your degree of success depends upon your dreams,
persistence, and the plan of action you put in place now.

Not every obstacle you face has a negative outcome. Very often you face change, which on the surface can seem to be a backward step. However, often it's simply conditioning you for something far better.

I've changed jobs and even found myself in brief periods of unemployment. On the face of it, they seemed like wrong moves. However, there are no mistakes in life if we learn lessons.

I knew in my heart it was part of my life and my ultimate journey to something far better so I accepted it. There were times when uncertainty crept into my psyche, but I kept going with a positive and optimistic attitude.

Throughout our lives we change our thought processes according to our needs, wishes, and aspirations. It's a perfectly natural response to the environment and its impact on our feelings about ourselves and our lives. This occurs on a daily basis when we have a positive attitude. It helps to sustain momentum and can occur as a direct result of opportunities which manifest. This could be something as simple as finding a parking spot outside a restaurant, catching a green light when we're in a hurry, or finding our car keys which we thought were lost. We also do it for more complex issues in our lives.

Not all change is positive, of course, and you need to understand the difference. Positive change is any alteration adding obvious value and depth to your life. There are often things we change for the wrong reasons, perhaps as a hasty reaction to a situation or stimulus or in response to something said to or about us. Quite often, it's only after we've made the commitment to that rushed change we realize we've in fact made the wrong decision.

Positive thoughts and actions create a positive reality.

If the changes you instigate aren't working, it stands to reason that you make alterations. It can be an ongoing process, but it is important for you to recognize the value of positive change. Adopt it when what you're doing is not working and you feel yourself going the wrong way on your life's journey. If you continue to do things the same way, I can assure you the outcome will be the same each time.

When you are on the right track, these changes are crucial components to the natural progression for enhancement rather than a simple reaction to problems.

When some things aren't working, change or modify them to suit your purpose (don't become disillusioned by the process or descend into a state of chaos). Change is an integral component in the phenomenon of growth and development, and with it come fresh new ideas, thoughts, and beliefs along with the consequential actions.

Change is a constructive way to adapt to your environment—the one you create yourself through positive thoughts, feelings, and emotions. It will help you grasp opportunities coming into your life every day. It all becomes part of our journey toward something more amazing if we only embrace the changes and use them for good.

Changing your life means making modifications to the way you look at yourself and the interaction you have with the many people, situations, and opportunities that arise on a day to day basis. It's the way you react to circumstances. Your look—your dress and overall manner. This includes your words and actions. Most of all, it means making the positive amendments to your attitude. This in many ways governs all aspects of your life—how you react and subsequently transform at those times when you think things are really not going according to your plan.

> When the door of opportunity opens, learn to keep it that way with an ever-positive attitude.

It's simple to look at life through a haze when things become gloomy and just as easy to view the many consequences of change through very negative eyes. One secret to happiness is looking at and embracing change when you accept it as a positive movement in your life.

The strength and courage of the human spirit is unfathomable—it's inspiring. With practice you can adapt to any change and use it as a positive and uplifting catalyst for your plan of action. You can have great results.

Accept and embrace change and understand the nature of and necessity for negative influences in your life. They can often accompany positive change and surreptitiously conspire to derail your efforts. When you understand that negative elements in your life also serve a very concrete purpose, you'll be less afraid of change and more accepting of those aspects ultimately molding the life created.

> Positive change represents the fresh winds of opportunity blowing in your life. Recognize them and welcome the incredible abundance that follows.

Build your framework for success on a platform of courage, strength, and determination to overcome the negativity and draw from them all the power and passion required to embrace positive change and allow it to permeate all corners of your being.

When you realize that change has the capacity to invigorate and energize your efforts, you'll do it as often as possible. Change to one small aspect of/in your life often means changes to every aspect. It becomes one important component to success.

That one tiny action can act as an extraordinary catalyst, working in a domino effect through many more areas of your life. Incredible and focused effort in one small aspect has a "butterfly effect" on the rest of your life and your future. This is a component of Chaos Theory—the mathematical supposition that small changes in one area of life can lead to profound alterations on a much larger scale.

It's imperative to ensure wherever possible that the changes you make are positive. Think them through, because you can just as easily make negative choices. They too can have a chain reaction through your life.

Advancement requires action. It becomes an ongoing process of evolution, and when used as a positive medium it can have a very beneficial effect on all areas of your wonderful life.

Positive change only comes about with the desire for betterment in your life.

LESSONS LEARNED

1. Change is inevitable—always ensure it's positive and in support of your dreams and goals.

2. Accept and embrace change and understand its true nature and value.

3. Change works as a butterfly effect across all areas of your life.

4. Utilize change to improve your circumstances.

5. Change has the capacity to invigorate and energize your efforts.

6. Instigate changes as often as necessary to improve your life and keep you on track.

7. Negative aspects will also accompany positive change.

8. Advancement requires action.

9. Negative elements in life also serve a purpose.

10. Change is an ongoing process of evolution.

Chapter 10

CHANGE YOUR HABITS, CHANGE YOUR LIFE

When you don't take steps to fill your life with
confidence and determination, you invite failure
into your world. It soon becomes a habit.

A habit is principally an action that becomes almost involuntary when performed enough times. Stop and look around at the many people who wallow in self-pity every day, often without realizing it. It's obvious that failure can become a habit. It turns into a prison with real walls—invisible boundaries defining and determining thoughts, emotions, words, actions, and the resultant failure.

We invite bad habits into our lives—consistently nurturing and stimulating them until we are totally locked in negativity in many aspects of our existence. When bad habits become the norm, it's difficult to divest ourselves of pessimistic behavior, and it begins to impact our lives.

We are affected by habits in one form or another every moment of the day. We do many things as a routine without thinking too deeply about them. When they're done for long enough, they become a ritual. The longer we support them, the more difficult they are to break.

Much of this is harmless and a functional part of living, such as rising of a morning at a particular time, washing, dressing, eating, and walking out the door at a precise minute. We catch the usual bus, train, or ferry to work (many of us walk, drive, or ride our bikes). We walk in, sit at our desks, turn on the computer, and check our emails. We go through the same routine when answering the phone. We have morning tea and lunch before we clock out and retrace our steps home. We have our evening meal, a shower, and perhaps, watch some television. Maybe we check emails and drop in on our social networking sites before it's time for bed, only to begin the cycle all over again. With a few exceptions and incidental detours, that's pretty much it for many of us (apart from those who have a social life—that too has aspects of habit about it).

> Your self-image and habits are interrelated. To improve one, set about adopting strategies to improve the other.

We all have bad habits—some worse than others—and often they serve to derail us from our journey. Identify and eliminate those with the capacity to bring you down. Learn to adopt those that are positive and have the capacity to fuel your push to ultimate success and abundance.

Bad habits serve no real purpose in our lives. They are blocks to success, and although they might start out as mere irritations, they have the capacity to take over our lives and act as barriers to our positive growth and development.

You identify them by the effect they have on your life. Begin by being positive in your outlook in everyday dealings with others, no matter who or what you encounter. This can be quite difficult, and you may need all your resolve in the beginning to get past the hurdles. Bad habits are adopted partly through laziness and at other times as a shield against the outside world. They act as fillers in our lives when we are idle or unfocused. They can develop into an easy path to follow when our journey is becoming too tough and we need something less threatening to hold on to.

Research tells us that it generally takes up to 21 days to form a habit, reinforced through constant thought and action.[1] However and in contrast, it can take a long time, a great deal of focus, and a concerted effort to break a habit, especially if it has been with you for a long time and requires a great deal of effort or intervention (such as smoking). We automatically attach labels to habits and spend a lot of time and money trying to rid ourselves of those that impact us adversely.

> If you want to maintain momentum in your life, ensure you have momentum in your goals. Make them as big and as colorful as possible.

Often we fail because it takes a lot of effort and real determination with no easy way to abolish those things that make us feel uncomfortable or get in the way of life's great enjoyments. They represent the path of least resistance, and while we refuse to acknowledge their challenge to our way of life or the impact they have on us, we continue to tolerate them.

With any pattern of behavior, it becomes a habit when there is some perceived upside. For instance, in adopting this "bad" series of actions, there has to be a positive aspect. This would be your link to the adverse behavior.

Eliminating habits is about choice. However, before you can do that, you have to first be aware of the habit and try and rationalize the downside. Next you will want to instigate the change and see some real value in doing so.

Having identified the habit (or habits) and understood the reason why you want to eliminate it (them), begin with one that's simple, such as biting fingernails. Replace it with a good or constructive habit and begin building it through positive action and affirmation. You see the value in changing your behavior, such as pride in having nicer looking, longer, and cleaner nails.

You should also write down your bad habits and be very honest with yourself. Begin with those habits you can easily identify. Now discover ways and means to abolish them and set a time frame for any assistance or intervention you could require. Also identify the positive side of eliminating these and replacing them with more positive and uplifting actions.

To take this action, particularly if you have some habits considered potentially life-threatening or dangerous, enlist the assistance of others with experience who can give you the support and encouragement you need on what could prove to be a very long and protracted journey.

There might be a need for greater intervention in changing some habits. Seek medical or other professional assistance with specific habits (such as smoking and weight loss) with the capacity to impact health or wellbeing. If in doubt, always seek assistance. There are many support groups available.

> To embrace success and abundance in your life, you cannot permit negative attitudes to destroy or cloud your vision of personal triumph.

Bad habits by their nature are adopted almost instantaneously and, unfortunately, require more time to break. Once you eliminate the negative, rapidly replace it with a positive. Be diligent and have faith in what you're doing. Understand why you require the change and firmly believe that it's a positive asset to your life.

Stay focused; support your forward momentum by writing your existing positive habits in your journal along with those you'd ideally like to have. It's another way to give your journey power, direction, and balance.

Positive and powerful journal entries will remind you of the path you took (and are taking) to reach your goals. They automatically become a comprehensive source of positive reinforcement in those moments when you feel vulnerable or in need of support.

> When you decide to open your mind and absorb all the knowledge and wisdom possible, you also make the unconscious decision to embrace success and abundance in all areas of your life.

Once you've identified the upside, you should then look at what you will be surrendering or losing as a consequence of adopting this behavior and eliminating those (bad) habits. You may be receiving something, but what are you giving up and what is the consequence of this behavior? For instance, think about what positive result you receive from adopting the (new) behavior and what you might achieve by changing your current habit/s.

Examine both sides of the argument, and you'll be in a much better position to make an informed choice. Once you've taken the steps to scrutinize all perspectives, the pattern will become less of an involuntary action, because you are now in a position, based on your conclusions, to make that educated decision of the side you wish to take. Do you now feel good about it? Is what you are receiving a better result than the one you're seeking to replace? That's the big decision.

Within three weeks it's possible to make the (sometimes difficult) choices to change habits. This has certainly been true in my case. During that three-week period, the mind is able to adopt the new patterns of behavior based on the enriching nature of the choices made. As a result, your mind accepts the new modifications and improvements with little interruption to your life.

> In making the decision to change my habits for the better, I'm in fact signaling my intention to add more positive light, color, and clarity to my life.

It helps considerably when you have some kind of "awakening." In my case, I came to fully understand and embrace my purpose. The thought of a future filled with assistance to others was the catalyst shaking me out of my slumber, putting my life on track toward something extraordinary.

Try to avoid slipping back into bad habits. This can happen during lapses in judgment and when you are under duress. This unnecessary pressure can also come from your detractors who show little faith in your commitment to your new and improved lifestyle.

If you're serious about the new you, it's important to embrace the changes enacted. Remember the reason they were accepted—to assist in adopting the new and more positive feelings about yourself. The alternative is the old behavior and the corresponding bad or negative feelings with the resultant impact on your life.

Very little thinking is involved as we go through our daily routine, almost as if we're on autopilot. They're called "the habits of everyday living," and we build our lives around them. It's only when they adversely impact us that we begin to consider them bad or negative. This can be as seemingly innocuous as biting our nails, putting our fingers in our mouths, showering in the morning rather than the evening, or drinking several cups of coffee at breakfast time. The list is literally endless, and there is no doubt they have the capacity to adversely impact our lives, though not to any real detriment.

> An acquired action will soon become a habit with acceptance through quiet affirmation and dedicated application.

Many of these habits require a great deal of willpower. There are, however, several things we can do and steps we can take to change our habits and put more positive energy and optimism into every day:

- *You must first want the changes in your life*: This means accepting them for your own reasons and not for other people. You have to believe that the change is a positive step in your life and worthy of your time and effort.

- *Commit your time and energy to the change*: Be determined to see it through. In spite of the uncomfortable feelings you may experience as a result of the changes, stick with the effort and remain focused on your goal of breaking them.

- *Tackle habits one at a time*: You won't become overwhelmed or disheartened during those moments when you might relapse.

- *Understand* how your habit affects you and realize any impact it could have on others around you. Does your swearing, public spitting, loud eating, lack of exercise, snorting, smoking, or over consumption of alcohol affect you? In what way? Does it impact others in some way?

- *Be aware of your habit at all times*: Know exactly what it is and how you wish to change. It's very important in the overall program.

- *Take action to change your habits and commit to it*: This is done by attempting changes one at a time. Anything else might overwhelm you and leave you disheartened when you lapse. You can stop the action immediately or do it gradually to reduce the possibility of adverse effects (such as withdrawals from smoking). Often the changes are more successful and less impacting when they are enacted gradually.

- *Be persistent in spite of the obstacles you may face*: You will come up against brick walls and it's important you remind yourself why you're doing what you are. Remain focused on the end goal and envisage the feelings of good health and happiness you will experience when the habit has been eliminated.

- *Constantly visualize yourself as a happy and contented winner*: Picture yourself free of the particular debilitating habits. "See" yourself experiencing the end result and the emotional freedom you will achieve through eliminating the old behavior and embracing the new.

- *Always seek support from others*: This might be friends and relatives, a coach or mentor on whom you can lean during those times when you're struggling. They can keep you motivated and on the right track. Professional assistance might also be necessary in some cases. The road will not always be smooth. However, if you remain focused and know beyond question your life can and will change through your new and vastly improved behavior, a profound transformation can occur.

- *Consistently remind yourself* of how things were prior to embarking on the new behavior, and keep the goal firmly in the forefront of your mind. When in doubt, be mindful of the reasons why you seek the change and keep alive the images of the new and invigorated you.

- *Reward yourself for even the smallest successes*: Do this during your quest and it will constantly serve to reinforce in your mind the fact you are on the right path and you are happy with the direction you're going. It will keep you upbeat and positive, especially during those times when you lapse.

- *Be aware of your relapses*: Don't dwell on them. Learn the lessons and resolve to do better tomorrow. If and when necessary, seek that professional assistance and guidance in breaking the barriers.

Changing habits will change your life.

NOTE

1. Steven Aitchison, "Develop a New Habit," Ezinearticles, October 13, 2006, http://ezinearticles.com/?Develop-a-New-Habit&id=326777.

Turning bad habits into good is like opening a window and allowing the fresh air of change to blow through your life.

LESSONS LEARNED

1.   A habit is an action that almost becomes involuntary.

2.   We're affected by habits every moment of the day.

3.   Habits can define our thoughts, words, actions, and, ultimately, our success.

4.   It generally takes about 21 days to form a habit.

5.   It can take much longer to break one, especially when it's been with you a long time.

6.   Always look at what you're receiving and giving up when altering your habits.

7.   It is possible to make (often complex) choices to change habits.

8.   Try to avoid slipping back into bad habits.

9.   We build our lives around "habits of everyday living."

10. There's a multi-step process to assist with changing habits:

- You must first want the changes in your life.

- Commit your time and energy to the changes.

- Tackle them one at a time.

- Understand how your habits affects you.

- Try and become aware of your habits and their impact on your life.

- Take action to change your habits and commit to it.

- Be persistent in spite of the obstacles you may face.

- Constantly visualize.

- Seek support from others—including professional assistance—when necessary.

- Consistently remind yourself of how things were.

- Reward yourself for even the smallest successes.

11. Be aware of relapses, but don't dwell on them.

Chapter 11

FIND REASONS TO SUCCEED— DON'T MAKE EXCUSES NOT TO

To find just one reason to succeed is worth
more than a lifetime of excuses not to.

In my early years, I found it so easy to make excuses for the various predicaments in which I found myself. During those dark times, I didn't see the point of working toward something I believed might never happen. Rather than put in the hard work I knew was necessary to find success, it became easy to sit back and blame other people and circumstances for my life. I did for quite some time.

I believe a lot of that poor attitude originated from my ten years of being bullied and constantly put down. I was never good enough and suffered mercilessly at the hands of peers. Though I was able to cure myself, a lot of the anger and frustration still simmered below the surface.

I did begin to wonder what else there was in life, what else the future held, and just how amazing it could be. After these periods of introspection, I decided to take a more proactive approach and do something positive for myself.

Since I can remember, I've always written quotations. Initially they gave me solace. I found peace in writing down my inner thoughts, not in a journal style of storage, but as third person writing in the form of quotations. My mindset began to shift, and as a companion, my life began to change.

With this new attitude I was able to release myself from the shackles which held me back. I began to find and embrace those very valid reasons to succeed. I began to put my "success blueprint" into place and started building.

Should you ever find yourself at a crossroads in your life, close your eyes, take a few deep breaths, and find the resolve to follow your heart to a wonderful destiny.

No matter who you are or what path your life is taking, there will be times when you want to just throw in the towel and walk away. Struggles will at times appear bigger and more depressing than they really are. It depends upon your state of mind as to how your life will be affected by the issues confronting you.

Success and abundance don't depend on your current circumstances. It's of no concern to your future what you earn or how intelligent you believe yourself to be (or others claim you are/are not). Irrespective of what resources you may or may not have at this moment, you can become incredibly successful and abundant at any time.

There could be some negativity in your history which might slow your progress in some ways. This would be due in many ways to your inherent beliefs, thought patterns, and the life you've lived and are currently living. That's the baggage which many of us carry through life. It can work as an anchor and drag you down and keep you there if you allow it to have power in your life. It can also be put to good use as a career accelerator.

Your future is based on the positive thought patterns you can develop from today and the passion and persistence you possess in the here and now and can harness from this point forward. Learn to take control of your destiny from this moment on; ensure you continue heading in a positive direction. Leave the baggage of yesterday behind and move forward with drive, vision, and enthusiasm. It's never too late.

> The only thing to fear in success is leaving mediocrity behind.

I always encourage my clients to stop and stand back—take time to look at the current situation and the impact the various issues are having on their lives. In these times when stress can affect judgment, it's important that rash decisions are not made.

Likewise, when the good times begin, don't become over-zealous or get a case of the jitters and make decisions you might regret at a later date. If you develop the mindset that your success is only fleeting, that's exactly how it will turn out.

Contrary to popular belief, it's not always fear of failure that clouds our judgment. Often it's a fear of success and all it implies. This can cause us to falter and close our eyes to opportunities. Once we learn to attract abundance into our lives, it can so easily change many things we might otherwise have taken for granted.

When the process of attracting money begins, you will have more freedom and consequently a completely different perspective on the world around you. You start recognizing greater opportunities and feel different about yourself. You'll soon have greater confidence and a whole new outlook as your self-esteem and feelings of self-worth continue to grow.

> When one door closes on you, don't waste precious time pondering the reasons. Begin looking for the new opportunities invariably presenting themselves to you.

I have read much about the so-called phenomenon of "tithing." It began in early times, where the general populous was expected to give one tenth of their industry/earnings to the Church, as a type of support. It was considered a form of taxation. Apart from financial support, this practice also included crops, fruit trees, various oils, and often the first born of cattle and other domestic stock. This in turn was used by the Church to feed the poor and disadvantaged in the surrounding villages and towns.[1]

In this day and age, we all have an obligation to give to those less fortunate in our communities. This giving should be free of expectation. We pay more than enough tax in all its convoluted forms, and therefore I don't believe in the strict interpretation of this practice (one tenth of one's income) as a general rule of thumb. It should be whatever you can afford.

Many consider tithing a means of cleansing the soul, making them feel good about their lives and intentions. It's true, but giving to others must be a spontaneous act rather than a means to make you feel good about yourself. That euphoric emotion will come automatically when you give freely and happily and without any expectation.

> Fill your life with smiles, not frowns; laughter and not tears; tenderness, not anger; giving, not taking; and happiness, not sorrow. For everything you give to others that's of yourself, you will receive back in abundance.

Everyday struggles make it impossible for many families to forfeit even a tiny amount of the household budget. It could be more sensibly applied to day-to-day necessities. Others, on the other hand, are in a position to give far more than one tenth of their wealth. Many have such a vast fortune, it would make no dent whatsoever in their business budgets or personal fortunes.

Giving one tenth of one's income is (still) practiced loosely in some religions and ministries. However, any form of philanthropy must come from the heart. It's a spontaneous and guilt-free expression of gratitude for everything that's great in your life. The act has the capacity to make a lasting impact on you as a selfless and compassionate individual.

Giving to others must result from a real desire to assist, rather than responding to some external pressure, either tangible or covert, or any desire to "look good" in the eyes of others. Those in a position to do so should give freely to the less fortunate. It's a real and emotive human trait bringing true rewards.

To give without expectation opens doorways to greater happiness and abundance. It removes greed from the equation and establishes a pathway to an even more incredible future for the giver, delivering feelings of warmth and contentment. To be truly successful, one must learn to share abundance and feel good doing it.

> When you decide that success is to be an integral part of your life, develop a strong plan of action with a clear and unimpeded vision of what you want.

Success has many fundamental implications. The very notion of the selfless tasks you can perform as a result of the abundance that can infuse your life should spur you on to extraordinary achievement in all aspects of your existence. You have at your fingertips the opportunity to truly make a difference in your own life and those of family members and friends. Equally importantly, you can also profoundly change the lives of complete strangers who do not have the drive to push onward to any reasonable level of success or abundance. They often feel unworthy or incapable of realizing it in their lives and are completely overtaken by feelings of hopelessness and despair.

This way of life invites success into your world and enables you to use it with wisdom, love, happiness, and gratitude.

> The joy of giving also allows the unbridled enjoyment of receiving. The circle of gratitude is complete.

Those who have the skills, creativity, and vision to succeed should do the best they can for both personal and altruistic reasons rather than continue a life of apathy. To suppress these traits out of a misplaced fear (of the unknown) is reckless and a little selfish when there are so many who could benefit from these wonderful gifts.

If you constantly base your decisions on the past, you will have no solid platform to create your future. There is absolutely nothing to fear from success—it makes the ordinary truly extraordinary and wipes the debilitating shadow of inadequacy from your world.

Once you begin with self-improvement and make the changes necessary to realize a very bright and successful future, you'll find the strength, courage, and vision to assist others on their individual journeys. This action of empowerment aids the ongoing development of your self-esteem and your feelings of self-worth begin to escalate.

If given a choice between the darkness of failure and complacency or the sunshine of success and abundance, in spite of the challenges involved I wholeheartedly continue to embrace the latter.

When you believe without doubt that you need only have unerring faith in yourself to see doors to greater opportunities begin to open before your eyes, you'll understand that it's not magic—it's life!

NOTE

1. Russell Earl Kelly, Should the Church Teach Tithing? A Theologian's Conclusions about a Taboo Doctrine (San Jose, CA: Writers Club Press, 2001)

Successful people are prosperous because they attract success and abundance into their lives through their passion, determination, drive, and vision. It doesn't occur by accident.

LESSONS LEARNED

1. Success does not depend upon current circumstances.

2. Prosperity is based upon positive thought patterns.

3. Struggles often appear bigger and more depressing than they really are.

4. Take time, stand back, and look at your current situation.

5. Never make impacting decisions when you're stressed.

6. Fear of success can and will cloud your judgment.

7. When opportunities begin to appear, your self-esteem and self-worth will grow.

8. With success and abundance comes real responsibility.

9. Never allow oppressive memories to dictate your future.

10. Any form of giving must come from the heart and be spontaneous.

11. Success breeds spontaneity and action in all areas of life.

12. There is nothing to fear from success.

13. Believe in the existence of success and abundance and doors will begin to open.

Chapter 12

MAINTAINING THE DETERMINATION AND INSPIRATION TO SEE YOUR PLAN THROUGH

When you make the life-changing decision to travel outside your comfort zone, you need neither a compass nor a tour guide. Passion and a steely determination become your driving forces.

I have always had plans for various things. I've constantly nurtured a desire to help people though for some time, I didn't quite know how. The notion of writing books to empower others was with me from an early age and always featured as a significant component of my plan. I have countless items I've written over the years and they all seem to revolve around the aspect of assistance to others.

I have written and produced a short film about empowerment in disability ('What if..?). I have developed treatments and synopses for various television programs. They are intended to empower and enrich the lives and futures of homeless people, the disadvantaged and disabled.

Real determination and inspiration bring opportunities to your door. That optimism and enthusiasm you have for your life can and does open the door wide and invite positive energy to be an integral part of your future. Having a plan is the easy part. To make it work, you must constantly apply equal amounts of determination and inspiration. For many, that remains the difficult component of the equation. If you've ever played a sport, built something, or taken a trip, you understand the necessity for a plan. For it to be a success, you must see clearly the need to execute it and follow it to finality.

It takes inspiration and determination to maintain a positive spirit and view your results objectively. You won't always get the positive outcome you want. However, if you stick by the steps outlined in this work, you will gain a greater understanding of how to attract abundance into your life and capitalize on the opportunities coming your way. This will allow you to create a life around the gifts you receive and move forward with confidence and determination.

In any good life plan, learn to take one step at a time. We all like a speedy result, but when dealing with something as complex and important as your future, you have to learn patience and be meticulous in your approach. By plotting, planning, and organizing, you can systematically check off one positive result at a time and move methodically through your list.

To remain motivated, especially through the difficult times, you also have to be passionate about what you're doing. Keep your goal at the forefront of your mind at all times, in spite of the problems you encounter. No predicament or obstacle will ever be so big that you can't find a way through, over, or around it.

> Make the conscious decision today to push boundaries and break barriers. Shout to the world your self-belief and resolve to succeed.

Getting bogged down with unrelated tasks, issues, and concerns can be an everyday struggle. However, by maintaining your drive and passion, you can more easily stick to your plan and have the drive to follow it through. Stop and think about why you are doing it. Know where you're heading and understand completely the prize at the end.

Sacrifices are inevitable. Embrace change—it too opens a window on your life, as long as it is positive and can assist you to achieve your goals. Remain focused and inspired, and above all never lose sight of the horizon.

> Always look at obstacles as signs. Like rain, problems bring with them a renewed freshness and a real and tangible opportunity for growth.

Sir Isaac Newton was a brilliant mathematician and physicist. He created his Third Law of Motion: "For every action there is an equal and opposite reaction." Every problem then has a solution, though it might take some thinking and working to discover the answer. Be persistent and you'll find it.

There will be those times when you hit a brick wall or your plans appear to stall. It will be so easy to become discouraged. You must learn that failure is part of the success process. Once you can objectively face disappointment and deal with it in a very positive way, you have a much greater understanding of the mechanics of the journey you've embarked upon. Any failures will be temporary, and success will be that much sweeter.

> The quickest and most direct route to success is found in one's self-belief. Drive and persistence to embrace abundance and a refusal to accept setbacks are simply fuelled by determination.

The rewards you receive depend upon the amount of effort you put into your tasks. When you feel depressed or confront an issue or problem with no apparent solution, it's paramount you remain focused, results-driven, and, above all, determined.

You can never allow negativity to bring you down or sidetrack you. It's crucial you look closely at the situation and take the time to see the problem from all sides and angles.

> When you know you are working hard toward your goals, don't allow a day to go by without having appreciation for yourself and your efforts.

Every journey has the capacity to impact you in a variety of positive and negative ways. It's important you allow yourself the time to rest and recuperate whenever necessary. Take time out to recharge your batteries. If you neglect your own welfare, you will be of no real benefit to others. No matter how focused you are, always set time aside to chill out and enjoy some down time. Good mental and physical health are paramount to your future.

As you overcome obstacles and your goal becomes ever closer, the entire process is like a journey on an aircraft across the globe. At some point during the expedition, no matter how excited and focused you are there is the real possibility of jet lag to bring you down. In terms of your personal journey of growth and development, I like to refer to it as "success lag." It really does have the capacity to diminish your focus, deplete your energy, and bring you down.

Continue to find that time for yourself—whether a sporting, creative, or social interest—to restock your energy levels and regain momentum. Stop, replenish, and return to the task. Your mind and body will thank you for it. You will work harder, longer, and more strategically when you have a clear head and sharp mind.

Your success won't suddenly vaporize during the time you take to look after yourself. Take time out for yourself and you'll be in a far stronger frame of mind and better physical condition to continue on the path to success, this time with greater steel to embrace your next incredible goal and continue on that amazing path to achieve your destiny.

> On those rare occasions you feel life's challenges are diverting you from your path, remember—first you dream, then you dig deep for the drive, passion, and self-belief required to fuel it.

Take one step at a time. A journey can take much longer than anticipated, so it's important you pace yourself to keep your energy levels up and any incapacitating feelings at bay.

Finding the drive should not be difficult if you've decided on something you really want to do. Be fired by the dream of a better, richer, and more fulfilled life. Those dreams and visions of something more fantastic than you ever previously thought possible should be the catalyst for this new and inspired you, to move enthusiastically toward that wonderful goal.

Whatever is in your mind and your heart is also at your fingertips.

Remind yourself every day why you're doing what you are, just why you have these great dreams, and exactly where you know your journey is taking you. Hold inside a real determination to reach your goals and be motivated by your dreams and visions of what you know you can and will achieve and the incredible color and passion that will fill every fiber of your being.

You must believe that this is the life you want to live and you are completely deserving of everything that's great in your wonderful world. Have absolute confidence in yourself and the life you're leading, and never underestimate the power of the human spirit. Two of the major limitations you'll face in life are your lack of imagination and your inability to believe in yourself.

Always reach for the stars. They are within your grasp. Success and abundance, like opportunities, are all around you, though in many different forms. Develop a positive and focused mindset so they are drawn to you like a magnet. They are in your life for the asking; you need only get yourself into the right frame of mind.

Success and good fortune know no cultural boundaries. They have neither religious nor language barriers. They are unique to each of us and manifest in whatever form we decide through our dreams, visions, and determination.

Start living that life today in the here and now—it will begin to take shape immediately as you focus on your desires and continue with each passing moment. To initiate this wonderful phenomenon called creative visualization (see Chapter 3), begin seeing yourself doing the specific thing/s at this moment, and continue that vision even when the path gets difficult.

There's a saying, first coined by Frederick R. Barnard: "A picture is worth a thousand words."[1] That's exactly the task underlying creative visualization. Believe totally in your wonderful life and the direction you're traveling. Allow yourself to see it in all its color, depth, and clarity.

Don't allow your focus to wane or wander, even in the darkest of moments. Make your thoughts and visions very colorful, positive, and upbeat. Forget about the past and start living in the present to create a wonderful, successful, and abundant future. Begin today—this moment—and build your ideal life. You now have at your disposal everything you require to be successful. Make up your mind to have an incredible future and begin manifesting.

Experience the fear of struggle, but never be afraid of adversity.

You will often need to work hard on yourself to maintain your high levels of inspiration and determination. There are several things you can do to achieve this:

- *Measure your effort* rather than the outcomes. This will keep you focused when you might otherwise have a tendency to feel deflated or lagged, or when you fall short of your expectations (often helped by the sometimes misplaced expectations of others whom you allow to influence you).

- *Maintain a routine* and record all progress in your journal. This allows you to gauge your progress and serves as a constant reminder of your incredible journey.

- *Enjoy what you do.* This will keep you focused on the task at hand and on track. It serves as a buoyancy mechanism during those moments of indecision/deflation.

- *Reward yourself.* A very important step because we all need a pat on the back on occasions.

- Enjoy the moment.
- Make yourself feel special when you achieve your goals, no matter how small they might be.
- Every achievement is a milestone.

- *Vary your routine/approach* to maintain interest/enthusiasm. This limits the occasions when you might become disheartened or lose momentum (in spite of your journal).

- Live and work to your own expectations and not those of others.
  - It's your life and your journey.
  - Set your own goals and measure your progress by your own means, without the interference of others (no matter how well meaning they might claim to be).

Master these key strategies and begin to understand the importance of inspiration and motivation in your life and how they work hand in hand to assist you on your journey. Always keep your eye on the prize and be totally determined and committed to success and achievement.

It's counter-productive to wish for an easier path in your life. Simply discover the energy and drive to do better. Life's challenges are neon lights, pointing through the doorway to a brighter future.

Believe in yourself and your life in spite of where you might be at the moment. Give energy and color to your existence as you move forward with passion. Self-belief breathes life into your world, adding value to your many projects. It serves to elevate self-esteem and drives you to even further achievements.

The greater the belief you have in yourself, the greater worth you attach to your life. Entertain self-pity in your world and you immediately empower failure and remove your drive and focus to achieve your dreams. Suddenly you'll find they're out of reach.

> There are three fundamental rules for success: Believe in yourself; believe in yourself; believe in yourself.

Sanction your positive thoughts and actions every day. Adopt the discipline and focus required to maintain your incredible journey, even in the face of apparent defeat. It will enable you to find within the drive to overcome any obstacles you encounter and eventually achieve all you desire.

Understand that your life can deliver many small victories every day, and you should recognize and celebrate these as they occur. Don't dismiss any achievement as trivial, luck, or just coincidence. Everything occurs in your life with a specific purpose.

Enjoy your life and continue to develop a future you want and deserve. Never allow yourself to become complacent or mediocre, and always—I mean *always*—be genuinely grateful for the wonderful things that occur in your life, no matter how small or insignificant you believe them to be.

Know that problems also arise as specific success building indicators, designed to make you aware that things can derail your efforts if you don't take the time to find plausible solutions. Remain balanced and focused. Do that and you're well and truly on your way to building a very strong and secure future.

You are the most important person in your life, and until you can fully embrace that notion and appreciate who and what you are, your inspiration and determination will not reach the heights they deserve.

NOTE

1. Frederick R. Barnard, in the publication *Printers' Ink*, December 8, 1921, page 96.

When self-belief becomes a way of life, others will have no option but to also believe in you.

LESSONS LEARNED

1. Equal parts of determination/inspiration will empower your plan.

2. Take one step at a time and be patient.

3. Keep your goals at the forefront of your mind.

4. No problem is ever too big that you can't find a solution.

5. Remind yourself of your incredible journey and goals.

6. Don't allow yourself to get sidetracked.

7. Constantly review your plan.

8. Embrace change.

9. Start living your life today. It will take shape immediately.

10. Hold on to your dreams and visions through difficult times.

11. Don't allow yourself to get discouraged.

12. Small failures are part of the success process.

13. Have quiet time to offset "success lag" and maintain inspiration.

14. Every day will bring small victories—celebrate them.

15. Achievement doesn't result from luck or coincidence.

16. Every occurrence in your life has a purpose.

17. There are specific steps to assist in maintaining inspiration and determination:

- Measure your effort rather than the outcomes.

- Maintain a routine and record progress in your journal.

- Enjoy what you do.

- Reward yourself.

- Vary your routine/approach to maintain interest/enthusiasm.

- Live and work to your own expectations and not those of others.

18. Don't allow mediocrity/complacency to permeate your life.

19. You're the most important person in your life. Fully embrace your own magnificence.

Chapter 13

THE VALUE OF PASSION
AND PERSISTENCE

Changing circumstances always present great opportunities
as well as new challenges. Once you recognize the difference,
you'll understand the need for passion and persistence.

I have encountered many problems in my life and just as many negative people.
On countless occasions I've been asked why I bother with the effort I put into
things. I've been told that success has passed me by and success has unfortunately eluded me. In spite of the negativity, I kept my enthusiasm, passion,
and persistence because I have always seen them as key elements in my life.
Without them, the future inevitably looks bleak.

Passion and *persistence* are two of life's most powerful drivers, especially
if you're seeking to attract prosperity into your world and accelerate your success. Decide on the existence you want and the plan of action you'll use to
realize your dreams. Embrace a positive attitude and fuel your journey with
the two Ps.

Simply dreaming about success will never make it happen. It's not enough
to just *hope* that life will get better—it won't improve to any great extent without foundation, and it will certainly lack longevity.

Decide to enact positive change, set your goals, and put your plan into action. Walt Disney put it so succinctly: *"All our dreams can come true—if we have the courage to pursue them."*[1]

A well-structured plan is imperative if you are to realize your goals or have any impact on your dreams and ultimately your future. It's only as good as the power behind it and the action taken to fuel it. It must outline a very positive and determined course of action.

You will never find adventure outside if you don't have passion and persistence within.

Ensure as far as possible that what you are seeing, hearing, and doing is totally harmonious with your goals and dreams. Remain focused and don't allow any negative influences to push you from your path. To give credence to the destructive words and actions of others is to deny yourself the crucial support, encouragement, and belief necessary for your forward journey.

Learn to adjust your perception of success and fill your existence with self-respect, determination, passion, love, and gratitude. When you load your life with positive responses to the problems confronting you during your every day, the path ahead will continue to beckon, and while obstacles will nevertheless present themselves, you will build the resolve to deal with them in a very positive way.

A first impression gives us our perception. It leads to a reaction, ending with a consequence. Be careful of what you think you see.

Live and breathe your desires; have them in the forefront of your mind every day, with specific time set aside to visualize your dreams and goals using the various methods outlined in previous chapters (see Chapters 3, 4, and 5). These powerful tools have the capacity to fire up your drive and focus and ultimately change your life.

You must love what you do. Discover and nurture a true purpose for springing out of bed every day with a smile and throwing yourself headlong into your work (with a real focus). Remain energetic, happy, and on track by making a list of the incredible things about your work and reading it every day. This is one of the most simple but effective ways to uncover your true purpose.

It is possible to achieve a degree of success through undertaking something which does not necessarily hold your imagination or warm you with passion. However, in order to stand triumphantly on the summit of your exploits and feel the warmth of success touching all aspects of your life, it's necessary to love every component of what you do. Know beyond question you are capable of achieving great things.

To release much of the negativity in your life, become involved in community work, join a social group, engage a neighbor in meaningful conversation, learn a sport, or take up a hobby. When you embrace a "leisure focus," it can take much of the spotlight away from the negativity you might otherwise be experiencing. It's an ideal way to re-energize yourself and renew your enthusiasm.

When you're being dragged down by something which neither inspires nor empowers you, there can be a lot more pressure on you. As your vision shifts and your outlook brightens, you can begin to see your life through new and much more positive eyes.

Broaden your mental horizon, look at your life from many different aspects, and become more engaged with the positive components of the world around you. Your attitude can now undergo a monumental shift.

Once you find a serious purpose in life, you will discover the drive and persistence to strive for constant achievement.

Albert Schweitzer was a theologian, musician, philosopher, and physician. He also won the 1952 Nobel Prize for *Reverence of Life*. He has been quoted as saying, *"Success is not the key to happiness...If you love what you're doing, you will be successful."*

True happiness, then, is a key to finding success, balance, and abundance in your life. Find and embrace it with exuberance, grace, and gratitude, and continue to build the incredible life you deserve.

In my first book, *The Unstoppable Power Within*, I touched on the aspect of action—massive action. Again I stress that any action you take should be massive. There can be no distinction. You must approach success and abundance in your life with enthusiasm and optimism. If you truly want *the* best, then you have to do *your* best—always. Make sure the action you take is aligned with your goals and dreams to keep them on track and prevent yourself from becoming disillusioned. Should that occur, then your dreams could fade into the darkness of despair.

Dreaming about great times ahead and tremendous abundance will always make you feel good. They have the capacity to warm you through, especially in those times when you feel uncertainty creeping in. They give you an anchor to the future you're building.

Keep these feelings positive and relevant by taking all the action necessary to keep them fuelled and powerful. Remain determined to see those dreams become a reality in your world. Don't sabotage them—support them through positive and focused action every day.

> Hold fast to an idea, plan, or project and ensure you nurture, cherish, and develop it through a strong and unwavering belief in your own ability.

You will find it so much easier to go that "extra mile" in your efforts to create a wonderful world for yourself and your family when you discover a true passion for what you do and fully embrace the faith and excitement underpinning your actions. Now you're driving forward to even greater heights.

When you derive enormous pleasure from your journey, you can more easily begin and end each day with a spring in your step and an unbridled enthusiasm for all aspects of your being. In spite of any obstacles you face, your faith in yourself and your journey will be the fuel required to sustain your forward motion.

> Never surrender your dream to another person or situation, but know that the intensity of purpose will grow in unison with the magnitude of the obstacles encountered.

Each morning, give thanks for the day ahead and manifest the great things you want to happen (I still advocate 15–30 minutes of quiet reflection wherever possible). Even some things as small as a parking space, a bus running on time, or a snag-free drive on the highway take just a few moments of introspection.

Likewise, no matter what time you choose to retire in the evening, wear a smile and embrace those feelings of true gratitude for all you've achieved during your day. Think of the successes you've had and fully embrace them. Believe your whole life is a success and your journey is taking you to an incredible place.

No matter how small, everything happens for a reason. Spare a few thoughts for gratitude. Try to adopt the habit of leaving your problems outside when you have your quiet time. Make specific places sacrosanct and problem free.

When you truly embrace what you do and enjoy every aspect of your interaction with others, your persistence, optimism, and enthusiasm will drive you. Understand where you're going and know that the effort it will take to get you to that incredible place can help you to remain focused and driven.

If you can truly see your future and embrace those feelings of success and abundance as they unfold, then you can derive enormous pleasure from everything you do. Those wonderful feelings of achievement fuelled by your drive and enthusiasm will assist you to more fully understand exactly what it means to have control of your destiny.

When you have a gritty determination and push forward with diligence, you begin to empower yourself and your journey. The phenomenon of attracting incredible success and abundance into all aspects of your life has now begun.

Each breath you take should bring with it the resolve to live an extraordinary life using all your skills, knowledge, drive, compassion, and gratitude. It's then you'll see your destiny more clearly and truly taste the fruits of abundance.

If you make the decision to constantly retreat from the reality of the actions required to succeed, you may discover you have some deep-seated issues keeping you from moving forward and realizing your goals. An inability to embrace and harness the drive and intestinal fortitude necessary to advance in your life should encourage you to seek the assistance of others who have forged a path.

Every day you take action to realize your dreams moves you closer to the threshold of your destiny—simply believe.

A coach or mentor is a very positive and focused individual with the power, experience, and vision to assist you to get your personal and professional lives back on track. They don't speak incantations or work some magic trick (although individuals who rediscover success after powerful coaching might disagree); these focused and driven leaders call on their experience, courage, vision, enthusiasm, and determination to reinforce in you the drive and focus required to realign your beliefs and subsequently grasp success.

You may actually do it without their help, but the assistance, guidance, and support they provide can keep you buoyant during those times when stress and doubt threaten to engulf you.

Once in total alignment with your beliefs, where you find them coming from a place of passion and excitement, you begin to discover the sunshine in your existence. You are in effect creating a perfect environment where abundance can flourish. Provided you sow the seeds and constantly nurture them with passion and persistence, you are maintaining a garden where success, abundance, and happiness can flourish.

> When you have dreams, persistence, drive, and gratitude in your life, success and abundance are drawn to you like a magnet.

Never lose sight of the big picture, and understand that every moment of the day into which you put positive energy and resilience is a step in the right direction in spite of problems and obstacles encountered. Persistence comes through one's ability to understand the nature of success. If you want something badly enough and you refuse to surrender, your persistence is the tool enabling you to forge forward toward your goals.

With passion and persistence for what you do and a yearning for success, equaled by the positive and practical steps taken to achieve results, your every day will logically be filled with incredible effort and subsequent gain. Each and every action you take will therefore be massive and give your journey momentum and longevity.

NOTE

1. Pat Williams and Jim Denney, *How to Be like Walt* (Deerfield Beach, FL: Health Communications, 2004), 63.

When you're truly ready to embrace success irrespective of your personal circumstances, decide to take that initial step; have the required passion, persistence, and drive; and clearly visualize every aspect of your abundance.

LESSONS LEARNED

1. Ensure what you're seeing, hearing and doing is in harmony with your goals and dreams.

2. Build the resolve to deal with problems in a very positive way.

3. Fill your existence with self-respect, determination, passion, love, and gratitude.

4. Love every aspect of what you do.

5. Have a passion and excitement for all that your life involves.

6. Ensure you understand why you're doing what you are.

7. Make the decision to put your plan into action.

8. Gritty determination leads to empowerment.

9. A plan is only as good as the power behind it.

10. Always keep the big picture in the front of your mind.

11. Live and breathe your desires.

12. Set time aside every day to visualize (fuel) your desires.

13. Every moment of positive thought and action is a step in the right direction.

14. Understand the nature of your effort and your persistence will be a key.

15. Align your actions with your goals and dreams.

16. Know where you're going and understand the effort it will take to get you there.

17. Always maintain your garden where success, abundance, and happiness flourish.

18. Your passion and persistence should equal your positive and practical steps.

19. Every action will be massive when your efforts remain focused on your goals and dreams.

Chapter 14

A POSITIVE ATTITUDE CAN MOVE MOUNTAINS

Abundance results from setting forth on a journey of self-fulfillment fueled by self-belief, gratitude, passion, vision, and persistence.

I have endured countless setbacks in my life. I've suffered under the weight of some almost insurmountable struggles and had to dig deep for the drive to continue: From those early days with the stutter and the relentless bullying, to almost drowning at age seventeen. I suffered emotionally with the death of my brother and many other incidents along life's path. I often wondered if the reward would be worth the effort.

On so many days I found it very hard to see daylight through the dark clouds which seemed to gather overhead with monotonous regularity. Those were the times when I wanted the earth to open up and swallow me. I just wanted to hide away and forget.

I made up my mind through each and every stage to keep going. I decided I had to remain positive in spite of what was occurring around me. It was difficult but possible because I listened to that little voice inside who was urging me on and soothing me. We each have it - the voice of reason and compassion—which speaks honestly to us in times of trouble and uncertainty. Too many of us dismiss it and take another, less prosperous path. If you adopt a positive attitude, you can literally do anything.

Dr. Norman Vincent Peale brought us his timeless masterpiece, *The Power of Positive Thinking*. It was first published in 1952 and is still in demand today. To have a positive and successful life, one needs to eliminate as much negativity as possible. This premise forms the basis of Dr. Peale's amazing work.

These words might seem at face value to imply an uphill battle for many of us and even appear implausible at times, given the various obstacles we face on a daily basis. However, it is possible to protect ourselves against negativity with a powerful and positive state of mind and the drive, passion, and persistence to rise above those "bring me down" influences that can hit us at any time.

Quantum physics tells us we are all linked to the universe, because we're all energy in some form. Positive thinking, therefore, is a fundamental component as thought is definitely a form of energy. Moreover, it's the power of thought that has the capacity to move us to confidently complete extraordinary feats.

A positive attitude has the power to enrich the whole person with warmth, passion, and gratitude for the wonderful things in life. When this becomes a normal part of our existence, we attract more and more opportunities—like attracts like.

When you embrace life and become attuned to what's happening, you'll know beyond question you have the ability and capacity to truly see, feel, and touch the great things starting to manifest in your world. You should begin to clearly visualize your destiny in all its amazing and intricate detail.

> With great optimism and a clear vision of where you want your future to lie, enjoy everything that life has in store and never allow mediocrity to be your mentor.

With clear and unambiguous visualization, each day becomes a more positive and realistic place. The whole process rapidly morphs into an indispensable part of your very being. It becomes an absolute and critical life force.

It is certainly possible to be successful and enjoy incredible abundance in all spheres of life, though you may on many occasions have to work very hard to achieve it (at times a real struggle when you want to surrender the fight and hide your face from the world). Maintain a positive mindset, stay focused on your goals, and know you are on your way to outstanding abundance. Build your dream based on these optimistic and results-driven visions.

Unfortunately, many of us have been taught from an early age that some things are impossible, no matter how hard we try. How many times have you been told you'll never amount to anything? Perhaps a well-meaning parent, sibling, guardian, or significant other has said that you really don't have the intelligence, height, sense of humor, looks, or know how to take on a specific job or sporting activity. You're not smart or creative enough to succeed. You don't have the money, drive, or resilience to do what it takes to be a success.

Often these comments are not made with malice but rather misplaced concern, yet with little thought to the long-term consequences of their impact on self-esteem and feelings of self-worth.

Irrespective of the cynicism from others—for whatever reason—hold true to your beliefs, plans, passions, and dreams. Jeffrey Gitomer said it best: "Ignore zealots. These people will try to rain on your parade...because they don't have a parade of their own."[1] He suggests we avoid them at all costs, and I happen to agree with him.

In spite of opposition, walk toward your goals with the determination and courage to be the best you can. Face adversity with a positive attitude. When you get knocked down, get back up. When you falter, regain your momentum. Should you encounter clouds and periods of obscurity, look for the openings and continue forward with passion and persistence. It will make you stronger and more confident.

One hundred years from now, it won't matter how much money I had during my life, how big my house was, or how fast I could drive my car. The total essence and power of my existence and the legacy I leave will lie in the positive and lasting impact I had on the lives of others.

As tough as life might sometimes seem, maintain a positive attitude and carry it with you into each day and every situation. It's a learned process, often in the face of overwhelming oppression. It can be achieved by holding on to your dreams, believing in yourself, and adhering to the plan you have in place. Remind yourself every moment of how far you've come and what a wonderful and abundant future lies ahead of you.

Ask yourself positive questions all the time and constantly reinforce your inner strength with powerful and optimistic responses. Keep the darkness at bay by elevating your spirit and remaining focused and driven. Compliment yourself for your wonderful life, and be colorful and happy when speaking about who you are. Surround yourself with positive people and things.

> You should never fear your destination if your map is clear, your efforts true, and you have an incredible amount of self-belief in your heart.

Rather than asking yourself why things are bad or why nothing positive is happening in your world, turn the equation around and look for even the smallest positive flame in your life. Begin the rebuilding process by telling yourself, "I'm so happy because I enjoy my life." "My world is full of love and happiness, and I like every aspect of my existence." "I'm very successful, and I'm paid a lot of money for my creativity and experience." "I have good health because I exercise daily and eat a sensible diet." "My life is improving every day because I have a positive attitude and I work conscientiously toward my goals."

Your responses will depend upon your perception of what opposes you every day, your positive and focused choices, and the blessings coming into your life—often in disguise. It's so easy to look with gloom upon the issues harshly impacting us and then complain when the cards seem stacked against us. It's human nature. "Thanks to the global situation, my job is no longer secure." "I don't feel there's a place for me in this company anymore." "I hate my job; it's so boring." "My life is down the toilet because no one seems to like me." "I wish I lived in a nicer house and drove a better car." The list of grievances can be endless as we continue to wallow. We can too easily find comfort within these walls of abject solitude we build around ourselves and our lives.

Turn this picture around and look upon these challenges as good things, rather than risk spiraling into the inevitable loneliness of self-pity. Seize this incredible opportunity to release the untapped genius lying dormant within. We all have it in some aspect of our lives. Begin doing positive things for yourself to turn your circumstances around. Stop, look, and listen. Scrutinize the situation from all sides and begin to breathe life into those notions and ideas snoozing some place in your mind or sitting dormant in your journal, waiting to be unleashed. Free yourself from the torment of recrimination and put your plan of action into play. Get the ball rolling on an incredibly prosperous future.

> Be grateful for every blessing in your life and never stop being happy, sincere, honest, and caring. Take the hand held out to you and learn everything there is to enrich your wonderful life.

The road ahead won't become suddenly paved with gold. It requires sustained effort, focus, and determination—often enormous amounts of each. You have to actually do something positive. You have to take action. There's no better time than right now when you think the situation is lost and you're at risk of falling into a dark chasm. Those feelings of abject misery leave you with nowhere else to go but up. Look around for the opportunities presenting themselves and grasp them. Do something amazing for yourself, your family, and your future. The results might even astonish you.

The application of positive and uplifting material to our lives can see profound changes take place when we believe fully in what we're doing and have absolute faith in our own abilities. There can be no middle ground when we have a firm belief in ourselves, our wonderful journeys, and our plans of action fueled with the courage, passion, and determination to succeed.

The moment we allow doubt to creep into our lives and affect our behavior, we've already succumbed to the crushing pressure of loss and failure. While we remain on this path, it will become self-perpetuating and eventually totally destructive.

> Defeat in anything you undertake is really a momentary state of mind. It's only when you decide to submit that the condition becomes permanent.

Take control of the situation and turn it to your advantage. With a shift in attitude, there are no limits to the opportunities presenting themselves and certainly no boundaries to what you can achieve. Your evolution from the person you are now into the successful and productive person you are striving to become depends upon the positive view you have of your life. It also hinges on the empowered and inspired approach you make in enacting the changes necessary to move forward with passion and purpose.

There will be occasions when you have people in your organization who may not be as positive as you would like. They might, however, be great at their job, and therefore you don't really have the luxury of terminating them because it could be detrimental to the business. You should also think of the impact such a move could have on that person's life.

It's important to visualize yourself liking that person and working well with them. Recite mantras such as, "What am I learning from (name)?" "What am I teaching (name)?" I like (name)—his/her company has a positive effect on me." Or, "(Name) is a great worker and a very good asset for this company." In time there will be aspects of that person's attitude changing, and you too will begin to see them in a better light.

Turn adversity into advantage. This can drastically alter your perception, adding color and clarity to your world. Learn lessons every day from both the positive and negative thoughts, words, and actions of others.

Opportunities come in a variety of guises when you open your heart and mind and believe in your ability without reservation. Accept them graciously and know they will enrich your life. It's now you will come to the realization that anything (and everything) is possible.

Hold in the forefront of your mind the knowledge that you are an incredibly loving, happy, bright, creative, abundant, and truly worthwhile person. You are the captain of your own success ship. Constantly remind yourself that the voyage you choose on the ship of your making will ultimately decide your destiny. It's then you'll have absolute clarity in your thinking.

> With energy, vision, dedication, and a firm belief in our own ability to rise above adversity, we will continue to build a better world.

I too have been told over the years by others (whom I believed to be my friends) that my chances of success had passed me by and I would never amount to anything; and of course I was too old to achieve anything meaningful in my life because I didn't have "what it took" to be a true success. These barbs hurt deeply because I didn't expect venom (and jealousy) from those I held dear.

I was able to shake the heavy feelings of sadness and distress. I knew in my heart I was growing more and more successful with each empowered day. The impact of those harsh words was actually positive as I was driven to greater heights. It fueled my determination to continue on my journey to find and embrace success and abundance in all spheres of my life.

Although I initially failed to recognize many of the countless incredible opportunities arising throughout my life to that point, due to the fact that I had blinders on, the wonderful times nevertheless far outweighed any sadness. I can now freely and confidently recognize and embrace those (once elusive) opportunities. I continue to express gratitude for the countless blessings bringing light, life, color, and clarity into my world.

Never allow circumstances to be an impediment to opportunity, nor attitude to destroy your access to personal success and abundance.

Negative influences of others have the capacity to impact you on many levels if you allow them. Apart from using physical force, no one can make you do anything you don't want to, although we often take to heart comments that should be relegated to the waste basket. These mind games can have a most destructive influence over our lives if we give them permission to ride with us. It's never in the best interests of success and abundance if we allow the negativity of others to hitch itself to our wagon.

So often, though, we receive this interference at a time in our lives when we are vulnerable and feeling low in our spirits. Those who endeavor to shackle us with the darkness of failure are themselves wracked with anger, fear, uncertainty, and frustration. They seem to be constantly driven by the demons preventing them from rising to any great heights in their own lives.

You might not yet know the exact route you're taking to find your success. As long as you know your destination and possess a steely determination to get there, you'll find the opportunities along the road to assist you to get to where you know you want to be.

Through surreptitious means to destroy your plans for success and abundance, these negative individuals continue their efforts to unload their feelings of low self-esteem and negative self-worth onto those of us whom they perceive as successful. Jealousy is a truly destructive and subversive emotion.

When you allow jealousy to influence your judgment, suddenly the green-eyed monster is sitting on your shoulder guiding your every move. It's unfortunately a normal human reaction when we feel under siege. It does nothing for our self-esteem if we are narrow-minded enough to affect others with the negativity we feel about ourselves.

Life is like a supermarket: Amid the hustle and bustle, it brims with wonderful and interesting things. Often, though, it takes some effort to reach the really special items on the top shelf, just out of sight.

So many people are skillful at unloading darkness onto others. They appear to thrive on this destructive behavior. They spend their lives bringing others down to their base level rather than expending a little energy raising themselves up to new heights.

Refuse to be one who views life through opaque glasses. The vague and distorted images you receive prevent you from building a clear, successful, and abundant life. As a consequence, you could spend your time wallowing in self-pity and continuing the destructive downward spiral. It's very difficult to achieve positive things in your life when you're constantly subjected to a barrage of negativity.

You must decide to prevent the destruction of your destiny by those who lack the drive, determination, vision, and certainly gratitude to realize any real future for themselves. Listen to the voice inside as it shouts your wonderful traits and constantly encourages you to lift yourself above the punishment of those who would gladly see you fail, only to sneer, "I told you so!"

Don't succumb to self-sabotage as a mechanism to silence outside voices. Your destiny always lies freely ahead of you and never in the hands of someone else who may continue to stand behind you and try to drag you back to their position of stagnation. Use your success to reduce the spiteful and destructive words of your detractors to simple whispers in a storm. Allow them to float off into oblivion.

I shall be well and truly on the path to enlightenment when I find the courage and vision to trust and embrace the voice inside.

Positive and empowered thinking is the incredibly effective mechanism to fill voids in our lives that might otherwise be repositories for negativity and darkness. We should strive to constantly consider life as the glass at least half full—rather than half empty in times of stress. We will know that we have an abundance of sunshine, opportunity, smiles, gratitude, love, respect, courage, determination, power, trust, truth, and support in all aspects of our lives.

In those times when we are troubled and feel dejected, the notion of the half-full glass assists us to grow and evolve in spite of the obstacles. We can recognize opportunity and move forward with courage and determination.

Living a full and successful life is about looking on the bright side. It means finding the joy and happiness in all manner of circumstances rather than the negativity (the anchor) in situations that can and will take (and keep) us down.

Nothing in my life occurs by accident. I am the master of my own destiny.

To constantly fill your life with positive thoughts requires a great deal of work. It means reminding yourself every day of the reason you are who you are and why you're leading the life you are. In spite of the negativity from your critics, it is important to retain that positive frame of mind and give yourself constant and ongoing encouragement. It has the power to end wars, build cities, create masterpieces, develop global businesses, eliminate poverty, and heal sickness.

Positive thinking is the most uplifting form of attitude we possess. It's one of the most powerful tools in your arsenal of life. Learn to harness the incredible energy found in your self-belief; put it to good use.

Every step you take on your journey to success will be fuelled by your attitude. Therefore, to remain focused and upbeat you must embrace a positive attitude and never allow the negativity of others to crowd your thinking.

As long as you understand that you have complete control of your destiny and you possess the right attitude, you should see great changes in your life within a very short space of time.

> The only regret you should ever have in life is that you didn't try. Should you try but not reach what you believe is your full potential, you will have succeeded because you have given your dreams your total focus and energy. That's a winning attitude.

Have faith in yourself and your journey. Fully embrace the skills you possess, the plans you develop, and the ability you hold at your fingertips to take you from where you are to where you want to be. Obstacles will always arise no matter who or where you are. The key is to recognize them and exercise your willpower to find plausible solutions. You must always have the faith in your ability to rise above adversity and move ever forward.

In times of uncertainty, go back to the basics and reacquaint yourself with the reasons why you are on your special journey. It's a good idea to engage with the invaluable material available to you, and watch the DVDs, read the books and attend the seminars to get you back on track and keep you traveling in the right direction. You can always join blogs on various success-related sites where you correspond with like-minded, successful people and systematically reignite the flame of enthusiasm. It continues to burn deep within.

> You will find truth in life if you look for it, faith if you believe it, respect if you earn it, and dignity if you embrace it. You are the sum of everything you believe yourself to be and the measure of all that you allow into your life.

It's never too late to do what's necessary to get back the positive energy and keep moving forward. The more affirmative action you take and positive information you obtain, the greater will be your conviction. It will help you to maintain your willpower—a fundamental tool for overcoming adversity and embracing success in spite of the turmoil you might face at various times.

An uplifting attitude for at least one aspect of your life will soon spread into every area, filling the many nooks and crannies and enveloping your whole life in a warmth and glow. When you enjoy what you do and give it your all, you will begin to notice changes occurring in other areas of your life.

This will positively affect your outlook, courage, drive, passion, persistence, generosity, compassion, understanding, patience, tolerance, and wisdom.

You can have a great attitude and enjoy harmony and contentment or be constantly downcast and moody and walk around with a chip on your shoulder. A positive attitude will see you walk in the sunshine and enjoy a better quality of life. It's not difficult, though it does take some work to remain buoyant in times of stress and frustration. Always endeavor to look on the bright side of life—the view is much clearer and more pleasant and the colors are far more vibrant.

> It's not the distance you travel which has the capacity to turn your life into an adventure. It's the attitude, passion, determination, focus, and gratitude you take along as companions. That company you keep ultimately determines the amount of success you enjoy.

Concentrate on the journey rather than the destination and automatically shift your focus to more positive aspects of life. The outcomes will take care of themselves. Don't waste energy worrying about what might be. Develop your plan, have the right frame of mind, and stay focused; keep a positive vision and attitude and you'll be in the very best position possible to recognize opportunities and attract and embrace success.

It's when you have this wonderfully upbeat frame of mind that you find the power and energy to face up to and overcome obstacles. When you have your total focus on the prize ahead, you understand how imperative it is never to allow troubles to consume you. Always look for the positive aspect of any difficulty you confront. This will give you the key you need to open the door to overcoming it.

> Self-belief is your unerring confidence in yourself and the path you're travelling in spite of the trials, tribulations, or problems you encounter along the road to success and abundance.

Irrespective of what occurred in your life yesterday, make each morning a new dawn and approach the day with a focused and positive outlook. No matter how you wake, the sun will still rise and set each day. Your new and empowered attitude will positively impact on your life and on the lives of those with whom you interact.

> Success and abundance commence as a state of mind as you begin to embrace your new life.

Get into the habit of leaving behind any chips, bad moods, anger, frustrations, troubles, and preconceived notions when you walk out the front door. Put them in the waste bin; they no longer have any relevance in your new world. Look at each day as a brand new opportunity to enjoy life and embrace fresh possibilities.

Even though you will more than likely encounter some problems on your journey, when you have a positive attitude you will not only have a clearer perspective of everything before you, but also more strength and power to overcome the challenges and turn them into opportunities.

If you constantly look at life through angry eyes, you will only attract negative energy into your circle. This will have a debilitating effect on your physical and mental health and never result in improved circumstances.

Constantly look for the bright lights in every situation. Be optimistic, driven, and focused, giving yourself constant support and encouragement. This leads to improved productivity and a strong framework upon which to create a very positive and successful future.

NOTE

1. Nikita Koloff and Jeffrey H. Gitomer, *Wrestling with Success: Developing a Championship Mentality* (Hoboken, NJ: J. Wiley & Sons, 2004), 182.

The one thing distinguishing today from yesterday and tomorrow is the attitude you wake with and carry through the day.

LESSONS LEARNED

1. Have the right attitude and the drive, passion, and persistence to rise above adversity.

2. The power of thought has the capacity to move us to extraordinary feats.

3. Stay focused and always believe you're on the right path to your goal.

4. Never listen to the negative barbs of others.

5. Always be positive and upbeat in your thoughts and words about yourself and your life.

6. Bring down the wall of solitude we build around ourselves.

7. See obstacles as opportunities and release the untapped genius lying dormant within.

8. Opportunities come in many guises. Accept them graciously—they will enrich your life.

9. Turn adversity into advantage.

10. Believe in yourself, and there will be no boundaries to what you can achieve.

11. Sustained effort and determination are required to make the future bright and fulfilling.

12. Positive thinking fills voids and builds bridges in our lives. Exercise it daily.

13. Remind yourself every day of who you are and why you're doing what you are.

14. Positive thinking is one of the most creative and powerful tools we possess.

15. Your attitude will fuel every step on your journey to success.

16. Embrace a positive attitude and never allow others to cloud your visions of abundance.

17. Each day is a new opportunity to embrace success.

18. Angry eyes only ever attract negative attitudes.

19. Continue to support and encourage yourself in all you do.

Chapter 15

KEEPING THE RIGHT
FRAME OF MIND

Opportunity will only pass by without stopping,
when we're not waiting in the right place, at the
right time with a positive frame of mind.

No matter what we do—whether on the home front, in business, sport, or during our leisure time—we will never realize the full potential of our plans and actions unless we adopt the right frame of mind. This comes from a desire to do the best with what we have in the situations we find ourselves. It means being constantly upbeat and focused and applying equal amounts of energy and dedication.

It's never enough to simply want something and expect it to be there. You can't imagine anything concrete or lasting in your life until you adopt the right attitude. That means being focused on what you have and what you want—where you are at this point and exactly where you want to be. It certainly is possible.

Look around at the number of successful people who come into and out of your life every day. Many have overcome incredible obstacles to find monumental success and prosperity. Like you, they had to find the courage and drive to move out of their comfort zones. It can often be a very lonely place.

> Motivation is the tangible driving force working externally—the carrot luring you forward. Inspiration is the fire burning deep within, driving you toward your goals.

Success doesn't occur by chance. It's not something that "just happens" to some people. You have to work at it, nurture it, and constantly tweak your system to ensure you remain on top of your plan. Gain a firm understanding of the steps necessary to attract ongoing abundance into your life and continue to infuse it into everything you do each and every day.

There are several great ways to keep up your drive and commitment and stay focused. Listen to, watch, and read motivational material as often as possible (certainly as often as necessary). Get into the habit of fueling your drive and passion to remain buoyant and inspired and keep the seeds of doubt at bay. When you feel them creeping into your psyche, where they have the capacity to take root and derail your efforts, turn them off and ignite positive thoughts and feelings.

Attend occasional seminars on subjects that resonate with what you want in your life. Absorb the information supporting your dreams. Make sure you put it into practice as soon as possible. You have to put them to use or they have no positive function. Attending countless seminars, buying the material, and doing absolutely nothing will amount to zero.

Learn from the experts who have experienced the highs and lows on their own journeys to success. Read the posts, join the mailing lists, send them emails, and ask questions. Seek their wisdom and be guided by the advice you receive as your own expedition unfolds. Above all remain focused, enthusiastic, and persistent and never lose sight of your goals.

Associate with positive people who always have success at the forefront of their minds. Surround yourself with those who have a winning attitude and tap into their positive energy and influence. Separate yourself from those who through their negativity seek to impose their pessimism on you. Constantly seek out the company of people who think as you do (or as you would like to).

Inspiration has the ability to move mountains. Once you decide on a road to incredible personal success and happiness, you should allow nothing negative to stand in your way.

Not every workplace is a positive powerhouse. When your work environment and even your boss are negative, try to find another job where you will feel valued. Until that time, find aspects of your current position that bring you joy and happiness and make your work space a brighter and more inspired environment (where possible pin up family pictures along with powerful and positive images and words). Continue to contribute wherever possible by doing your job to the best of your ability, and ensure all your thoughts, words, and actions continue to be relevant and success-oriented.

When you begin to associate with motivated people, you'll feel the wonderful effects on all aspects of your life. Frustration and negativity can lead to failure if you don't take positive steps to redress the imbalance and fill your life with prosperous thoughts, feelings, emotions, words, and actions.

Finding and enjoying success is not simply a matter of closing your eyes, dreaming of a million dollars, and waking to find yourself covered in paper money or discovering several gold bars under your pillow. You can't just wish for the car, the holiday house, or the perfect partner and (*kapow!*) expect it to materialize in your life. Nothing is as simple or naïve as that.

If we could just make a wish and manifest whatever we want, everyone would be closing their eyes and instantly creating incredible things in their lives. This would make life an arduous and rather mundane existence. When you have everything handed to you on a silver platter, you run the risk of becoming blasé and conceited. Where there's no effort, there's no struggle and, therefore, very little appreciation for the wonderful opportunities and subsequent results arising from dreams, passion, focus, and hard work.

> The problem with success is often the perception of the work associated with achieving it. Too many people become disheartened or disillusioned as they look upon it as a chore rather than a blessing.

Achievement is the result of an exact formula. One fundamental ingredient is the power of the mind, and it depends upon the way you use it to achieve your results. Daydreaming alone will not open doors. Wishing will not bring success and abundance closer.

Most of us constantly "hope" for a better day. It is quite often used in a negative sense, because when we don't have the right frame of mind or we encounter problems, we *hope* things will turn out okay. We *hope* we might one day win the lottery. We *hope* everything is alright and that we'll emerge unscathed at the other end of our current uncertain situation.

According to the former New York City mayor Rudy Giuliani, "Change is not a destination, just as hope is not a strategy."[1] Hope does not positively empower us. When it stands alone, it has no influence. It's too often used as a measure of desperation. "I hope things get better." "I hope I find a job soon." "I hope my life gets better soon." "I hope my health improves." We too easily cling onto the word when we're in a rut or desperate for improvement.

Conversely, it's also a very powerful and endearing word, instilling in so many a real ray of sunshine for a better and more optimistic existence. When we add life to the word through a very sanguine and colorful frame of mind, we are providing a depth to our very existence. Without hope, we really have nothing upon which to pin our expectations. This positive and life-enriching word also implies faith in ourselves and the path we're traveling.

Real hope (when coupled with faith) is a positive and driven energy capable of facilitating incredible things. It can feed the starving and give aid to the developing world. It can provide clothing and education. Hope and faith can erect shelters, hospitals, and places of worship. It engenders courage, optimism, and compassion in those for whom all can seem lost at some given moment in time. It enables us to remain focused and on track in our quest for the ideal existence.

Hope is the torch that lights the flame of courage and determination. It drives us ever forward toward our goals. It provides succor when we feel at our most vulnerable. Never lose sight of hope in your life, no matter the impacting circumstances or the prevailing situation you face. Power it with an unerring faith in yourself and your ability with the solid belief that you are moving in the right direction.

When we have real faith in ourselves and a hope for a brighter global tomorrow, barriers have a habit of coming down, communication improves, and resistance is diminished. It becomes that positive force enabling us to rise to challenges. With an unfailing faith in everything we do and all we undertake, hope becomes the ubiquitous light at the end of the tunnel.

Success eventuates when the goal is fueled by a clear and unimpeded vision, driven by an unending persistence.

The whole notion of instigating success in your life should be approached in a regimented fashion. Like any venture looking for a solid and impressive outcome, you have to apply equal quantities of hard work, energy, and great determination. You must always keep your eye on the prize and formulate your plan according to your requirements. Maintain the constant and unwavering attitude of a successful person, and keep a bright and happy outlook on life in spite of the obstacles you may face.

The right frame of mind means being positive with absolute faith in yourself and your ability. Know without doubt that success and abundance are your birthrights. You are entitled to them. This fundamental outlook must form an integral part of who you are and what your life represents.

When seeking transformation in your life, begin with attitude. Once you have the right frame of mind with the drive and vision to move forward, success will become part of your future.

Maintain control of your journey at all times, thereby denying others the ability and/or opportunity to steal (or alter) your dreams. I call them *dream thieves*. We all have them in our lives and at some time have suffered at their hands.

When I was at school there was a saying: "Sticks and stones can break your bones, but words will never hurt you." If you have ever been taunted in your life, you know this information is far from accurate.

In one way or another we've all experienced the crushing effects of harsh words on our self-esteem and feelings of self-worth. They adversely impact us when our defenses are down and we're feeling vulnerable. We only have to remember with great sadness the many suicides occurring in recent times through the senseless bullying from those who lack respect or compassion for things for which they have little or no understanding or tolerance.

On the other hand, we all know and have experienced the profound and uplifting impact positive and endearing words can have on us. When spoken by those who seek to provide assistance and give us the motivation we need to find our own path in life, they become invaluable and enlightening.

While many of these individuals are well intentioned, they are nevertheless making a judgment on your life according to their own values. They react to your plans according to their own inherent ideals, fears, and doubts. They automatically apply their rationale to your life and view your dreams through their eyes, their beliefs, and their shortcomings.

Negative people appear to enjoy a lifeless existence in their narrow and lonely world of misery. They lack positive self-expression and seem to derive some bizarre delight in their ability to constantly put us down and criticize our drive and commitment. Our plans of success will never be their blueprints and they react accordingly.

These same people will tell you they have all the answers to your life's problems while their own worlds remain devoid of passion, color, and extension.

> When you share your dreams and visions with only a small number of like-minded people, you are ensuring the integrity of your plans and finding the support and encouragement often required to embrace success and prosperity in your life.

These individuals can always tell you why you will fail and sneer at anything you say or do, often because it's at odds with their own constricted view of the world. They constantly shy away from any challenge and are their own worst enemies.

The first real step is to make the decision to shut their interference out of your life. Once you do that, decide to fuel your journey with their residue negative energy. Their impact will diminish and their influence will fade into obscurity. You become unstoppable.

I always advise clients to share their vision with only a limited number of compatible confidantes. The more people you tell, the more likely you are to have your dreams, visions, and plans derailed by unhelpful remarks (your ideas could also be stolen by others). If you don't remain confident, the result can often be a loss of focus and deviation from your path.

When you allow the very limiting viewpoints of others to impact your plans, in effect you adopt their beliefs and surrender your passion, drive, and commitment. You no longer have control of your dreams and goals.

Ensure the group you build around you is in total harmony with your core values and desires. You must all contribute to a common purpose. Each person supports the other through a shared notion of success and prosperity.

Exercise trust in the support offered by others, but in general conversation try and retreat from sharing all your plans and visions (especially with strangers), unless you have absolute faith in them. Remain true to yourself in relation to your destiny as others could endeavor to steal your plans and, in so doing, deconstruct much of your future. Only trust those who share the same sunshine as you and who are in absolute harmony with the direction you're traveling.

> Assistance comes when we're most needing. Accolades come when we're most deserving.

It never makes sense to boast about your plans. Until they come to fruition, they are simply dreams and visions and can be easily taken away by those with the means to capitalize on the ideas you espouse. Never put yourself in the position where others think of you as a "gunner"—someone who is always talking about "gunner do this" and "gunner do that."

When you walk to the beat of another person's drum, you are allowing them to compose your melody of life. It will soon become the tune you follow blindly, until you make up your mind to break the constrictive bond and move forward according to your own dreams, visions, and values.

This is your life and your journey. When you hold your plan in the forefront of your mind, you can control everything that makes your incredible voyage worthwhile. You are the architect of your future. Build it to your own strict specifications and take your life in the direction you wish to go.

Remain upbeat, focused, driven, and ever optimistic that the life you're building and the journey you're taking is a path destined to deliver the success and abundance you so richly deserve. By keeping that very positive approach, you've already begun the process right now. It begins with a strong and unwavering belief and continues as a transformation into the reality you create with your own optimistic and focused thoughts and your treasured goals and dreams empowered by positive actions.

> Surround yourself with positive people and always insist they check their egos at the door.

There is never any better time than the present to begin living that ideal life. Irrespective of the fear and trepidation you feel in stepping out of your comfort zone, do it initially with cautious optimism, then with a resolute determination to achieve your wonderful goals. Fuel your dreams and visions with passion and drive. Keep them alive with the knowledge that your wonderful new life has begun, irrespective of obstacles faced.

See it, feel it, and know it's within your reach, because it's happening here and now. You truly begin to see and experience the color, warmth, and wonderful success in your life you deserve when you start to believe it.

NOTE

1. "Who Said 'Hope Is Not a Strategy'?" YourDictionary, Origin of "Hope Is Not a Strategy," accessed February 18, 2015, http://www.yourdictionary.com/.

Depending upon your frame of mind, you can view obstacles either as the diamonds they are or simply as lumps of coal.

LESSONS LEARNED

1. The right frame of mind is paramount in every aspect of your life.

2. Listen to, watch, and read motivational material as often as possible.

3. When doubt creeps into your psyche, ignite positive thoughts and feelings.

4. Attend seminars on subjects that resonate with what you want in your life.

5. Learn from the experts.

6. Remain focused, enthusiastic, and persistent, and never lose sight of your goals.

7. Associate with positive people who always have success at the forefront of their minds.

8. Seek out the company of like-minded people.

9. Find aspects of your job that bring you joy.

10. Make your work space a happier and more inspired environment.

11. Do your job to the best of your ability.

12. Have a plan of action and the determination to see it through.

13. The power of the mind is a fundamental component of achievement.

14. The right attitude allows you to maintain control of your life and journey.

15. Allow your life plan to take you in the direction you wish to go.

16. Beware of the *dream thieves* who try to bring you down.

17. Avoid the negative influences of those who seek to reduce you to their level.

18. Always remain upbeat, focused, driven, and optimistic in all areas of your life.

19. Harsh words can impact adversely on self-esteem.

20. Positive and endearing words can have an uplifting effect on our lives.

21. Never lose sight of hope in your life. It lights the flame of courage and determination.

22. A positive frame of mind allows you to live in the moment and begin your future today.

23. Success and abundance are your birthrights.

24. You will begin to see and experience success and abundance when you start to believe it.

Chapter 16

EMBRACE GRATITUDE, HAPPINESS, AND ALL THEY IMPLY

My gratitude, love, and optimism dictate the positive
and lasting impact I have on others on a daily basis.

Money does not bring happiness! How many of us have heard that adage over the years? For so long I heard it repeatedly from both the church and my father. It was a concept which I fully embraced for quite a long time. After all, it had to be right if my dad and the church told me so.

It didn't take me long to realize that those words were completely untrue. Surely, not everyone with money is evil. When I look around I see all the good which so many people do with money. The church too would be unable to feed and care for the poor without consistent funding. They receive it through the generosity of others.

When I was able to shake those feelings, my life took on a brand-new meaning. I found I could release myself from that negativity, allowing me to see and embrace gratitude, happiness, compassion, generosity, faith, and hope. It's those extraordinary gifts which are delivered to us on a daily basis.

In my experience, those disempowering words are generally espoused by the people who have no money. They're the individuals who lack the means, the drive, or the vision to acquire any and are generally in a rut. They constantly wonder how to pay the bills, keep a roof over their heads, and put food on the table. They complain about life and all their trials and tribulations. They float along on the sea of apathy, offering a string of excuses for their predicament as they look for sympathy from anyone who will listen.

These are often the people who seem to lack drive and ambition. There is no real inspiration in their lives. They appear to suffer soul-destroying low self-esteem and are content to sit back and watch the world pass by their very narrow and unproductive worlds. Through their ignorance and lack of vision, they do their best to pour cold water on your plans.

Without giving much thought to the effort necessary to accomplish a reasonable level of achievement in life, many people cannot see any great successes ahead of them because they have failed to plan and organize. They're unable to dream big enough. They lack faith in themselves and therefore have no vision of the true essence of success and abundance.

These are the same people who have an opinion on just about every topic. They consider themselves fountains of knowledge and wisdom concerning things about which they know next to nothing. We all have people like that in our lives, and without thinking of the consequences we allow their intrusion to impact us unfavorably.

These wise and knowledgeable individuals can tell you what you're doing wrong and just why you're failing. They can tell you what you should and shouldn't do and how to achieve success in all things. At the same time, their own lives are virtually empty. Opinions are the most abundant resource. Everyone has an incalculable number.

These people generally have quite a constricted viewpoint on life and never realize any level of intuition or creative thinking in their narrow worlds. They could have all this and more if they only took the time to plan and organize and, above all, have absolute faith in themselves. They tend to be disconnected from any reality and for all intents and purposes appear content with their lot in life. How can they possibly be content?

> Criticism of others is a clear indication of our belief in and support of our own mediocrity.

Money alone, of course, is not the answer to all life's problems, although it has the capacity to invite happiness, goodness, and a degree of stability into our lives. It brings with it a positive attitude and allows us to live a more comfortable and debt-free existence. Money allows us to travel, live wonderful lives, start and maintain successful businesses, and buy nice things for ourselves, our family members, friends, and even complete strangers. However, we must also learn to respect it and use it wisely and compassionately.

When we have money in our pockets, it certainly helps in times of struggle and uncertainty. There are also other components of life crucial for balance and harmony. They include love, gratitude, compassion, knowledge, trust, commitment, understanding, respect, good health, courage, patience, tolerance, respect, and trust. When we couple all of these together as part of a life-building program, we suddenly have the tools necessary to achieve a real level of success.

It's time to lose that often inherent fear of stepping out of your comfort zone. Rather than putting any real effort into life, like so many others throughout history have done, it's far easier to sit back and criticize those who have the vision, drive, and passion to take calculated risks and realize incredible abundance.

> Never live under the debilitating shadow of "if only." It automatically signals your inability to accept yourself as you are. The barriers to success and abundance are already forming.

Plan and organize your life and, when criticized, keep the faith in your-self. Retain your vision and leave your detractors in their own stagnation as the world and a vast number of opportunities rush by their world, eternally shrouded in darkness.

To obtain money and also pass through the other wonderful phases in our lives, we must follow a very positive and functional program. I believe the balance is fundamental to creating a truly abundant life.

Simply by adopting a positive attitude—becoming much more motivated (and inspired) and having the courage to embrace change in their lives—those with closed minds could otherwise have in their hands the ability to attract untold success and abundance and change forever a self-perpetuating cycle of defeat and misery.

> The key to success is to constantly strive to achieve those things which challenge you and to have true, heartfelt gratitude for the opportunities constantly filling your life.

Self-belief and the courage to embrace opportunities in the face of adver-sity is the first step on the road to great things. Achievement only comes when you make the conscious decision to do something positive with your existence.

A person can have an adjustment of attitude and begin to understand that good things can happen in their world every day in some capacity. This also applies to those who might to this point have considered themselves to be "bad luck magnets." Suddenly they have the ability to change their view on life. The only curse they carry is a lack of self-belief and ignorance of a more fulfilling life.

These individuals with disheartened attitudes about life simply invite negativity and seem to wrap themselves in it like a security blanket. They only feel satisfied when their lives are in turmoil and they can shout from the rooftops, "I told you so!"

When you let go of those preconceived, unhelpful notions festering deep inside, you come to the realization of the goodness in your life. This leads to feelings of gratitude, peace, and harmony. They invoke joy, love, and happiness with the ability to literally move mountains.

You won't achieve incredible success and financial independence if you fail to have gratitude in your life for all you have and all you are yet to acquire. Gratitude need not be wailing or gnashing of teeth. It can be done in the shower, in front of the mirror, at the dining table, or on the bus.

Gratitude is simply a quiet yet sincere "thank you" for all life's blessings. No matter where you are or what kind of life you lead, there are many wonderful things you should be thankful for. Search for them.

To succeed in the face of adversity is the sweetest prize of all.

This can, of course, be something as small as a smile from a neighbor or someone who gives up their seat for you on the bus (these days, that might be a bit of wishful thinking!). Perhaps you have an unexpected windfall or even find a parking spot right out front of where you want to be. The sun, the rain, cool breezes, and the birds that fill the air with song. Smiles, warm hugs, kisses, and handshakes. Good health, a roof over our heads, and the kindness of others. These are some of the things we should be thankful for every day.

The list of great moments is endless; they give us instances of joy and happiness and make us feel good about ourselves and our lives. That notion also includes those obstacles that serve to divert us to a more productive path.

Every day has wonderful moments where we're touched by the "blessing angel." During these incredible periods, take some time to say "thank you." They form an integral part of creative visualization. *Have I mentioned what an amazingly powerful manifestation tool it is?*

At the beginning of your day, stop and think about all you want from the hours ahead. Offer gratitude for the way you *know* it will turn out. You need not drop to your knees and lift your eyes to heaven, though it's not to be ruled out if you feel inclined to do it.

Speak your gratitudes each day and believe them. "Thank you for the successful meeting today." "Thanks for the signed contracts on the house." "Thank you for the safe drive today." "Thanks for the great friendships made." "Thank you for the nourishing meal and sunshine." "Thank you for the great business deal." The list is infinite and need not necessarily be related to incredible, earth-moving changes or events.

See these wonderful occurrences in all their glory. Experience the moment in detail—the color, warmth, and feelings associated with the wonderful successes. Know how you feel at these times, and don't be afraid to truly embrace the emotions.

Use the same practice of an evening when you give thanks for the great day you've had in spite of a few setbacks endured. Even though some things might not have gone as you had wished or planned, create a very optimistic attitude by being grateful for the day. It sets in motion a very focused and positive mindset.

Spare some thought for those things that didn't go according to your ideal plan. See how they might have helped by setting you on an alternative path. They can change your stance about specific issues and prepare you for even greater achievements in some other aspect of your existence.

> When you begin and end each day with positive and focused affirmations, you surround yourself in a warm glow of inspiration, and the hurdles you encounter won't seem quite so overwhelming.

Once you believe your future to be a reality as you see it, you'll begin to experience it. Always ensure those views are positive, bright, and warm, and never allow the darkness of doubt and fear to block your view of the horizon. It can be spectacular, with all the colors of the rainbow if you only take the time to be happy and have gratitude.

Apply the principles of gratitude to your everyday thinking. The notion of prayer need not conjure images of religious dogma. Instead, and if it makes you more comfortable, see it as a word simply implying your ability to stop and think about all that's magnificent in your life.

> I am worthy of abundance in my life and accept success and empowerment with gratitude and an open heart.

Know beyond question you are rich over and above your dreams—in love, happiness, success, good health, internal calm, and money. Embrace a clear understanding of everything that makes your life overflow with prosperity.

Most of us aspire to what can be termed the perfect life. It might not always eventuate exactly as we envisage it, but we do nevertheless have the ability to create something akin to magnificent. The power rests with you and in you. Don't allow it to forever lay dormant.

The positive and focused responses you offer to the problems in your life remain the many valid reasons you have for being the person you are. Problems occur in the lives of all of us to varying degrees. They primarily serve to make us stop and think about what we're doing and the impact of our behavior on others. I don't know too many people who are infallible.

> The more positive and focused you are about your journey, the greater influence you have on your life and the many aspects that have the capacity to bring you tremendous joy and happiness.

Never forget who you are and the exceptional work you do to be happy and successful. Always find the time and inclination to congratulate yourself. Have genuine gratitude and happiness for your own innate gifts of love, compassion, self-respect, creativity, determination, generosity, tolerance, and the countless achievements brought about by these priceless talents.

Hurdles in our lives are in many ways positive and functional tools. We should examine them in the light of the changes we make to our lives and our behavior and our impact on others and the environment. Feel and display genuine gratitude for them. Remember that after the storm, there is always sunshine, and no problem or issue looks quite as bad in the bright light of day.

When you learn to congratulate yourself and show true gratitude for small victories, greater successes will begin to flow more easily into your life.

Gratitude is a fundamental component of happiness. It's a tool that opens the door for greater achievement and abundance. It can't be faked; it must be a genuine and heartfelt emotion originating from a desire to improve your life through a process of sharing and displaying a genuine concern for others. It's the true deep-seated thanks for the wealth in your own life.

Take control of your journey and fill it with effort, devotion, and real joy. You now have an agenda of self-enrichment where gratitude becomes an authentic and self-sustaining part of your psyche and helps you push your life to even greater heights.

Congratulating yourself for achievements is also a big part of the process of attracting success and abundance into your life. Everyone deserves accolades for success, and giving yourself a pat on the back is a strong way to show support and encouragement for your efforts. It also enables you to consciously recognize the wonder and excitement in your life.

Fill everything you say, think, and do through every possible moment of your existence with bundles of gratitude, happiness, love, self-belief, power, and passion. When you can do this and have an immense faith in yourself and the path you're on, I have no doubt you will soon see the doors to an abundant future opening before you.

Every day brings a renewed confidence in myself through the knowledge that I am incredibly important and my life is worthwhile and enriched with love and gratitude.

LESSONS LEARNED

1. Money has the capacity to invite happiness into our lives.

2. Financial gain and all it implies brings a positive attitude.

3. Success is measured by a blanket of abundance, including money.

4. Change your attitude, increase inspiration, and find the courage to move forward with plans.

5. Fill your life with gratitude to begin the process of embracing success.

6. Apply the principles of gratitude to your everyday existence.

7. Problems arise in our lives to make us stop and think about our journey.

8. Gratitude is a genuine emotion and can't be faked.

9. Happiness and gratitude are ideal tools with the capacity to open the door to abundance.

10. Always congratulate and reward yourself for your achievements.

11. Happiness, love, and self-belief help to expedite the arrival of your wonderful future.

Chapter 17

GIVE YOURSELF PERMISSION
TO SUCCEED

Life is the greatest and most fulfilling journey we
will ever undertake. Our magnificent destination
we create ourselves is the bonus.

For so long I just didn't understand the need to give myself permission to
be successful. What does that even mean? I certainly didn't know anything
about it as a young boy growing up in the suburbs. I didn't understand
the philosophy. Surely life is measured in seconds, minutes, hours, days,
months, years, thoughts, words, emotions, and actions. What else could
there possibly be?

I convinced myself that all the stumbling and falling—the obstacles and
challenges—were just my lot in life. I didn't understand, particularly in my
early years, that the mindset I have and attitude I carry determine the future
I build. What's that all about?

So many of those early years were spent hiding away from the world and
everything that I believed was impacting me in a negative way. I had no interest in giving myself permission. I simply wanted to get through each day. It
was my struggle, and I certainly didn't need permission for that.

Once I realized that I was the creator of my own destiny, the fog of uncertainty began to clear. I started to understand the concept, and I realized I could give myself permission to be and do anything I wanted. It meant freedom, good health, happiness, friendship, and success. I wanted the ability and capacity to share my positive feelings with others. I gave myself that permission. Doors began to open before me.

It didn't mean there was an end to the problems I faced, but with a more positive mindset and an optimistic approach, the impact wasn't so severe or long lasting.

There's no doubt that outside influences can and do impact your life every day. However, success is not just about *what* you do. It's also paramount you have the right thoughts, feelings, and emotions about success. Understand what it means in your life. It will assist you to evolve as a person and understand exactly how it touches your life and the lives of those around you.

It's important to really understand just how the power of success will manifest in and enrich your life. It can assist you to change and grow based upon those positive feelings and emotions.

William James, the American psychologist and philosopher, wrote the immortal words: *"Be not afraid of life. Believe that life is worth living and your belief will help create the fact."*[1] From an intellectual family and with an exceptionally probing and creative mind, Mr. James was a very deep thinker from an early age. His studies lead him to believe firmly in the power of the mind to create abundance in all areas of his life.

It was Mr. James's firm conviction that by changing mental attitudes an individual is possessed of the capacity to change the outer aspects of his/her life. How powerful are these thoughts and words? They were devised over 100 years ago, during a time in history when free and lateral thinking was only just finding the bright light of day.

Until you make up your mind to be successful, that magical destination will continue to elude you. Make a promise to yourself to take advantage of every opportunity coming your way and actually do something positive to accelerate prosperity in your life. It won't occur by accident. You have to actually make up your mind to be a success and give yourself permission to be extraordinary.

> When you realize the infinite potential in life, give yourself permission to embrace prosperity and make up your mind to be an extraordinary human being.

Humans are truly fascinating creatures. The majority strives for greatness in every undertaking. We work hard (generally), play to the best of our ability, and as a rule do our utmost to aspire to an acceptable level of success. Unfortunately, given the nature of the beast and the various instincts we have, we are often prone to self-destruction on many levels.

Attitude plays a large part in our lives. Whether we choose to be positive and upbeat or make the decision to be negative and downcast, it will play a monumental role in the life we live and the future we enjoy. It can be bright, colorful, and exciting or alternatively dark, hollow, and uneventful.

We can choose to react adversely to impacting factors and adopt a negative stand, or take the path that ultimately delivers great opportunities and much more abundance. It is a choice we make.

> There is nothing I cannot achieve as long as I keep the flame of self-belief burning brightly inside of me and fuel my journey to incredible success with passion, persistence, vision, and gratitude.

Life's not a level playing field. Whether you like it or not, so many things can and do conspire to keep you down. The trick is to stay alert and surround yourself with as much positive energy as possible. When you are out there in the real world endeavoring to make a success in all spheres of your life, you begin to understand the nature of the many challenges faced every day. More importantly, you open your eyes to the incredible opportunities offered to you in many areas of your life.

Very often, however, we're blinded to these prospects as we focus on the things that are going wrong and don't give credit to the things going right. It's so easy to do this when our troubles seem to overwhelm us and make us feel as if the whole world is the enemy.

Every aspect of what occurs in life carries both positive and negative elements. When times are tough, it's much easier to focus on the negative. We seem to slip so easily into the realm of self-pity, doubt, and darkness. Without realizing the ramifications of this behavior, we automatically fall into the trap of despair and remain there. It has suddenly become the norm.

First and foremost, you have to believe in yourself as a person. You are a good, wholesome, and empowered individual who is working hard and creating a better life. Then, as a career-oriented individual—someone with skills, creativity, and promise who strives for the very best in their business practices and dealings with others. If you lack integrity in these areas, you'll miss balance in your life, and success and abundance will ultimately evade you.

Life is composed of various components that infiltrate and impact upon our every day. We have social/personal/family time and we have our business commitments allowing us to build a well-rounded existence for ourselves and those we love.

When we are able to achieve an acceptable balance so no area of our lives suffers, we begin to see growth, development, and abundance across the broad spectrum of our world.

You cannot build a lasting foundation of success and harmony on the stepping stones of yesterday. Rely only on the opportunities given to you today and the efforts you continue to make to establish a strong and secure base to ensure you remain focused on the road ahead.

Believing in yourself means having faith in the person you are. Know beyond any question you are on the right path to success. You have to develop and maintain the courage and strength of your convictions and the intestinal fortitude to realize them irrespective of any opposition you might face.

Self-belief means "carrying a flame" for yourself and the life you live. It means supporting yourself and having deep appreciation for the efforts you put into creating something special. You must have unswerving confidence in your plan and the actions you take to see it through.

You are incredibly important. Have true and unshackled love for yourself. It becomes a measure of your self-worth. It's one of the most difficult tasks and requires work and dedication. Support your values at all costs. When you feel worthy, you also have improved self-esteem. You know you're a good person, deserving of success and abundance.

Have you ever stopped and looked at your life and thought you were exactly where you believed you'd be at this time? Do you rate your performance as great, good, okay, less than inspiring, or needs a lot of work? Is your earning capacity as high as you believed it would be? Is your life as fulfilled as you *hoped* it would be at this time?

Until you understand what's not working in your life, you won't know how to change it. Think of those in the world who earn incredible incomes. What is it that makes them stand out from the crowd? Do you believe your thought patterns are as direct and powerful as theirs? Would you have the same mindset as they do? Do you occupy the same immense space in your life as they do in theirs? Would you have the same positive thoughts as they do? Are your dreams and goals as big and all-encompassing as those of the individuals who continue to make a positive impact on others?

> When you have total and absolute belief in yourself, nothing can stand in the way of your success.

Lose the self-limiting beliefs and step out of the shadows. Understand that you can create the ideal reality and enjoy a lifetime of incredible success and abundance. Have faith in the choices you make and begin to put your life back on the path to unlimited prosperity. Reposition yourself on that once seemingly elusive road to wealth, good health, and happiness.

Your income and lifestyle are directly proportionate to the choices you make in life based upon your beliefs. Introduce a system of change now, and understand that all things are possible provided you believe in yourself and have a strong and focused, all-inclusive plan of action in place.

When you come to the realization of the value and power of your own incredible existence, you will begin to believe that you deserve all the wonderful things that can and will come your way. This fundamental aspect of your being allows you to radiate your worth to others like a heater. You indicate that you have enormous respect for yourself and your life. It's this wonderful kindness that will draw people to you in all spheres of your life.

You become like a magnet when you radiate love, courage, happiness, drive, compassion, gratitude, tolerance, and understanding. It's in these moments that you occupy a greater space in the world and indicate to others the depth, color, and power of your inner Self.

Always focus on the task at hand. Sports coaches, mentors, and business development professionals constantly instill in their charges the fundamental necessity for focus. Your destination in life is the point ahead on the horizon where you should focus *all* your energy and attention.

Work optimistically toward your goals. Don't be dissuaded by the words and actions of others. Refuse to allow the small hurdles to turn into insurmountable obstacles. Don't allow them to push you from your ultimate goals. Use them as stepping stones to a great new and exciting life.

Fill your day with positive energy. Know your prize. Believe in yourself. Create your dreams and visions, and be determined to overcome any obstacles as you move systematically toward success on a very positive and structured plan. Above all, have profound gratitude for everything that occurs in your life. It's destined to take you to that magical goal where your existence will be full of color and vitality.

Gratitude is a fundamental key for opening doors and allowing abundance to flow into your world. It's as simple as saying a real "thank you" for what takes you closer to your goals. Blessings, like daily challenges, come into your world for a specific purpose. Examine your life and your reactions. Embrace the opportunities and accept the blessings as the gifts they are.

> Success is not the measure of what you have. Rather, it's the totality of the person you are and the sum of the opportunities you've grasped on your journey of life.

Remodel your life from today. Add passion and purpose to everything you think, say, and do. There is a reason for all things, and though you may not understand at the time what that could possibly be—given the impact outside influences can have on you—move forward with drive, purpose, gratitude, determination, and an unerring self-belief. Add these to your plan and don't allow any negativity to impact your life. The world will become your oyster when you make up your mind to remove the blocks and give yourself permission to stand out—to grasp opportunities. Do that and there are no longer any reasons why you should not embrace success.

There is absolutely nothing you can't achieve if you believe in everything you are, all you do and say, and continue to work with and add to the strong, colorful, and positive plan you have in place. Think of all the reasons why you are moving forward in spite of the obstacles you face and simply say, "I'm on my way to incredible success and prosperity."

Continue to look forward and remain positive and upbeat even through those dark moments when you become nervous and unsure. Regret should not be given any oxygen whatsoever. It has absolutely no positive place in your world. It's a negative and destructive emotion. It serves no purpose in your journey to your chosen destiny.

NOTE

1. William James, *The Will to Believe* (TheClassics.us, 2013), 62.

Always listen to that inner voice of reason. It will guide you on the right path. Set your goals, establish your guidelines, color your dreams, and listen with an open heart.

LESSONS LEARNED

1. Outside influences impact your life every day.

2. Positive thoughts, feelings, and emotions are crucial for success.

3. Life is not a level playing field.

4. Make up your mind to be successful.

5. Always give credit to things that are going right in life.

6. Believe in yourself as a good, wholesome, and empowered person.

7. Give yourself permission to be extraordinary.

8. Balance will assist growth, development, and abundance across all aspects of your life.

9. Feeling worthy will greatly assist your self-esteem.

10. Always focus on the task at hand.

11. Work toward your goal with purpose and determination.

12. Give power and passion to your actions.

13. Don't be dissuaded by the words and actions of others.

14. Gratitude is a key—it opens doors and allows abundance to flow.

15. Add color and purpose to everything you do.

16. Understand what's wrong in life to enable changes to be made.

17. Learn to lose the self-limiting beliefs holding you back.

18. Move forward with drive, gratitude, courage, and determination.

19. Add color and purpose to everything you think, say, and do.

20. There is no hurdle you can't get over in life.

21. Believe in yourself and your life and just do it.

22. Regret can have no place in your new and empowered world.

CONCLUSION

Looking at life through rose-colored glasses is like
living in a glass bubble. You can never touch and feel
the reality and passion of success after challenge.

Now you're beginning to understand the secret to success. Of course, there is none, because anything in life is possible if you work hard and want it badly enough. Perhaps your parents told you nothing was easy and you had to work incredibly hard for everything you get in life. That is still true to a degree. However, life today is made a little easier than what was endured by our predecessors. The Internet and new methods of communication now bring the world to us. Everything you want is at your fingertips. You need only know where to look and what to look for.

If life was a real pushover, everyone would be doing it. They're not—so it isn't. Life is certainly not a walk in the park, but it is made easier when you have a notion of a better life and a plan of action. It takes time, money, and energy to realize the dream of a great future. You have to remain determined to succeed. Stay focused on your dream at all times and understand what's required to achieve it.

Anything in life is possible, provided you plan and organize for it. You have to understand that you will face challenges every day—personal and professional. You will have days when you wish the world would swallow you up and other days when you stand proudly on the pinnacle as you have triumphs. Understand that it takes a whole lot of ingredients to make that celebration cake.

> Once you get out of yourself and into your dream, it will suddenly become your mission.

Every journey begins with that dream of a better life. That's the first step, and without it you may as well stay exactly where you are. When you can dream of something better, you can begin to put the pieces of the puzzle together. It's at this point you're on your way to an extraordinary new life. Don't let go of the reigns, and never surrender your view of the horizon. When the going gets a little tough, always remind yourself why you're working so hard. Develop a thick skin and an even temperament. If you give up and walk away, there will always be others ready to take your place, and if they are hungrier than you are, they take the baton and suddenly your future becomes theirs.

Every moment of every day is a separate step on your journey. Whether small or large, when you're moving in the right direction, you are doing what's necessary to grasp success. Every day will be filled with small wins, and they should be celebrated.

> Always believe in yourself and have trust in that voice inside, because when you need decisive and life-changing action in your life, the only voice that truly matters is your own.

There's no better time than right now to get moving. Don't just sit around pondering your navel. There's a great deal of work to do. You have to now begin to put the principles into action. Your great future will begin when you make up your mind to build something you want. It's a future holding your deepest dreams and desires. A great life only manifests when the right action has been taken and you stay focused and passionate.

Read the book from cover to cover and use it as a reference each time you need some motivation. There will be times when you fall off the track. Just simply take a breath, recover, and get back to where you're going. Understand that you are the only person who can live your awesome life. You are also the only one who has that unique voice inside telling you that you're a wonderful, happy, balanced, and courageous individual.

There are countless opportunities which arise every day to satisfy us all. Irrespective of who we are or what our backgrounds might be, we each have special talents we can explore. We simply have to step out of our comfort zones on occasions and go for it.

The detractors will always ask why and the response should always be, "Because I can too!" There are no reasons to accept mediocrity in life. There are no reasons to accept mediocrity from others. If you give up and walk away, you will never know what it means to taste success after challenge. The more times you get knocked down and stand right up again, the more reasons you have to continue on that incredible journey.

Kieran

> Never allow the clouds of uncertainty over the life of another to inadvertently or otherwise cast a shadow across your own successes.

A DICTIONARY OF EMPOWERING WORDS FOR EVERYDAY USE

Irrespective of how dark your past might be, it's the canvas of the present that is important, because it's those colors and hues which you take into the future.

Abundance: Means success in incredible amounts. A great quantity of everything which makes up our prosperity, whether good health and happiness, money, material wealth, or any other aspect of success.

Acceptance: Is your ability to embrace a person or situation, often in spite of the ramifications. It speaks volumes about you as much as the other person or circumstance.

Accountability: Taking responsibility for your words and actions and their impact on others. Step up and accept liability; have the courage and fortitude to answer ethically for your life choices.

Acclaim: Is praise and compliments for things well done. You can never accept compliments from others until you can easily accept them from yourself.

Admiration: The regard you have for another individual and that person can have for you in terms of the good you do and the respect you have for yourself and others.

Amazing: Incredible, startling, wonderful, and marvelous. When something takes your breath away and makes you feel fantastic.

Appreciation: The admiration, pleasure, and approval you have for the positive things touching your life and the reasons why things occur as they do.

Brilliant: When a person or situation is dazzling, just spectacular—simply shining and sparkling.

Charity: Giving aid and assistance to other people. It is a giving from the heart without expectation and with a genuine respect for the feelings of others.

Clarity: The precision and clear insight of a situation. What you bring to your life and a given situation with focus, drive, and determination. When you remove the peripheral information and leave the clear and unimpeded vision of your incredible life and journey.

Color: The light, lift, and freshness in your world or any given situation. That breath of fresh air breathed into your journey to add a whole new dimension to your life.

Commitment: Your pledge to succeed. The promise or vow you make to do your best to achieve your goals.

Compassion: Sympathy, kindness, and consideration toward others. Having a true concern for the welfare of other people and an empathy with their position.

Congruence: When everything in our lives comes together in unprecedented accord, with all pieces fitting snugly together to give greater unity, clarity, and color to our individual journeys.

Contentment: Those feelings you have of satisfaction, happiness, pleasure, and gratification when you know you are on the right track to great prosperity. It is the warm and endearing feelings you have about yourself.

Courage: The nerve and steel to act on our convictions in the face of the overwhelming odds we often face on our forward journey. Standing up in the face of adversity and doing what we know is right.

Destiny: Your fate or providence; a destination you desire to reach that brings with it abundance and prosperity.

Determination: Your willpower and tenacity in respect of a situation. Your resolve to stay the distance through an unerring belief in yourself and your life in spite of the obstacles and negative circumstances you may face.

Dreams: Those aspects of your life that drive you forward. The foundation upon which you build your incredible future. From your dreams come the color, clarity, and passion to continue on that incredible journey.

Drive: It compels you forward to achieve your goals. That inner force pushing you on even during those stressful times when you feel as if you want to quit.

Ecstasy: Far stronger and more powerful than any drug. Those feelings of love, bliss, rapture, and pure excitement when you realize your world is a wonderful place to be and you can enjoy every moment of your wonderful and empowered existence.

Empowerment: The inner strength we discover when we have victory over adversity in our lives.

Enchantment: A time of fascination, charm, and delight when we feel balance and harmony in our lives.

Encouragement: The selfless support you give others in the pursuit of their goals. The enthusiasm you show for their drive to be the best they can in their lives.

Enlightenment: The period of clarification and illumination in our lives when we finally see the power we have over our existence and feel comfort with the strong and unerring belief we hold in ourselves and our individual journeys.

Enthusiasm: Your keenness, fervor, and passion for a particular situation. That inner spark driving you forward toward your goals and dreams.

Esteem: The respect, regard, and admiration in which you hold others, they hold you, and you hold for yourself.

Ethics: A program of personal moral principles—a blueprint for our lives. Those just and decent rules of conduct governing our lives and the way we interact with others.

Exhilaration: Those feelings of happiness, excitement, and joy when you can see and feel the sunlight of opportunity and success shining in your life and you have warmth and love flood over you.

Fabulous: Where a situation is tremendous, incredible, magnificent, and extraordinary. Things are simply perfect, and you are in harmony with the world around you. Everything is marvelous.

Faith: The ability to believe firmly in what we're doing and the path we're traveling in spite of what others might say or the problems we may encounter along the way. The inner assurance we are doing the right thing for ourselves and our families.

Fantastic: Where a situation is almost beyond belief. It's truly incredible and above all expectations.

Focus: Your inner spotlight you shine on the road, task, journey, or action ahead. The concentration on any situation to assist in reaching a satisfactory conclusion.

Generosity: A kindness without expectation. Giving freely from the heart, especially to those less fortunate.

Goals: Principally your ambition, aims, and targets. It's the light at the end of the rainbow we all constantly strive for.

Goodwill: The benevolence you have toward others. The kindness you show without expectation. The care and support you show toward all manner of people regardless of their relationship to you.

Gratitude: Is a heartfelt thanks for things received. A true appreciation and gratefulness for a positive and warming situation.

Happiness: The feelings of elation we have when we find our life is taking us in the right direction, when we overcome obstacles and achieve our goals. It has the capacity to bring a smile to our faces.

Harmony: The accord and synchronization we have in our lives when everything is in total balance.

Honesty: A sincerity and truthfulness that should never impact negatively on others. A frankness and openness with the ability to heal wounds, build friendships, and assist others to grow and flourish in spite of challenges faced.

Hope: The eternal optimism we hold deep inside for a better world and greater personal existence in spite of the challenges and obstacles we face. The driving force that springs forth and empowers us to continue on our journeys in spite of the hurdles we encounter.

Incredible: A spectacular person or amazing situation, almost beyond belief. Someone or something that fills you with absolute joy and happiness.

Insight: Those inner feelings of "knowing" regarding a specific topic or matter, giving us an edge.

Joy: Feelings of elation when we're touched by something wonderful in our lives, bringing flooding feelings of warmth.

Knowledge: That awareness and understanding of what we're doing; the true insight into the power of our goals and a unique perception of the value of the life we're leading.

Longevity: Is your durability and endurance. That ability to maintain the level of empowerment, drive, and commitment in your journey.

Love: The wonderful, warm, and all-encompassing feeling of contentment and acceptance we find in a non-judgmental relationship with ourselves and others, in spite of our flaws and shortcomings.

Magnificence: The brilliance and radiance which shines from a particular person or situation. That specific aspect making the difference between ordinary and extraordinary.

Morals: The principles of conduct governing our everyday lives. There is a vast distinction between what is right and proper and what is incorrect, wrong, and inappropriate, especially in our dealings with others.

Openness: Laying yourself open to scrutiny and giving freely of your skills, experience, and respect. An honesty and sincerity attracting others to you.

Optimism: The cheerfulness, openness, and buoyancy you have—generally in times of stress or overwhelming pressure when you can retain your vision and focus in spite of what is thrown at you.

Optimum: The best possible and most favorable level in regard to achievement. The best of the best.

Passion: An excitement and enthusiasm for what we do. An inner driving force giving us the power and determination to achieve our goals.

Patience: Tolerance, persistence, and fortitude in spite of the trials and tribulations faced daily. Your ability to stay the distance and find plausible solutions to the problems you face. Nothing is insurmountable.

Peace of mind: The calmness and serenity enveloping us when our lives are on track and we know beyond question we're traveling in the right direction.

Perception: Your insight into and awareness of a particular situation. Your "knowing" and alertness to those things that can impact you.

Perseverance: Your resolve and determination to go the distance in spite of the challenges you may face along the way.

Persistence: The tenacity and doggedness you can muster in the face of overwhelming odds. The commitment to the challenge and sheer determination to achieve one's goals.

Phenomenal: Where something is extraordinary, exceptional, and unique. It can apply to a situation, opportunity, thought, or action.

Pride: Those overall feelings of tremendous satisfaction, pleasure, and delight we have when we at last realize the enormity of our achievements, the strides we've taken, and the path our incredible life is now traveling.

Prosperity: Wealth, riches, richness, and affluence. A birthright of us all, irrespective of current means or circumstances.

Purpose: Is a reason or intention. Your purpose in this life is to do the best you can with the skills you have and the determination you hold to be incredibly successful in spite of what life might throw up at you.

Recognition: That aspect of success bringing you accolades and attention for your good work, success, and/or generosity. The positive way others perceive you and respond accordingly.

Remarkable: When a situation is just outstanding. When what you do, see, and hear is just so special and astonishing.

Respect: The admiration and esteem in which you are held by others and that same deference you have toward them.

Responsibility: Taking ownership of your words and actions and their impact on others. Being accountable for what you do in life—ensuring your behavior is moral and above reproach.

Sanguine: Confident, optimistic, cheerful, positive, and upbeat. How we should all try to feel every day to empower and inspire ourselves to even greater achievements.

Self-esteem: Your degree of confidence in yourself and your ability to rise above adversity, to accept challenges, and to acknowledge triumph over adversity.

Self-respect: Your decision to respect yourself and be the best you can in spite of life's challenges. Others will never respect you if you don't respect yourself.

Self-worth: The sense of worth you hold for yourself reflected in the amount of love and regard you have for who you are, the life you lead, and the way you positively interact with others.

Success: An achievement, accomplishment, or triumph. That awesome objective we all strive for. An intricate component of our goals. The pot of gold at the end of the rainbow.

Terrific: Describes a wonderful situation. Everything about it is excellent—quite remarkable.

Thankfulness: Showing gratitude and appreciation for all that's great in life. Being heartily thankful for everything adding color, depth, passion, and meaning to life.

Togetherness: That feeling of warmth and acceptance in a union—whether immediate family, neighbors, local community, or global. It means being in a union with like-minded people where there is acceptance and a focus on a common vision. Everyone and all things in harmony.

Tolerance: Your acceptance of a person or situation. Your ability to remain level-headed and enduring in spite of any differences or misgivings you may have.

Tremendous: Fantastic, remarkable, incredible, terrific—the way we should describe our lives every day.

Triumphant: Proud, victorious, successful. How we feel when we've done something truly exceptional.

Trust: A firm belief in the honesty and respect of others. It comes from an understanding of our own worth. The total ability to move forward on our own judgment and courage to act on that intense feeling of "right."

Truth: A fact, reality, or certainty in a situation. It means to be open and honest in dealings with others. It brings its own rewards.

Understanding: Being considerate, thoughtful, and accepting of others. Having a kindness for the feelings of others. Being perceptive of the needs of others.

Verve: The vitality, energy, and spirit you put into your life. It adds drive and passion to your every moment.

Wealth: The affluence, prosperity, and abundance found in an empowered and enriched existence.

Wisdom: The accumulated mental power from living a complete and meaningful life. A real, unique, and in-depth understanding of what it means to truly comprehend the world around us.

Wonder: The magic and splendor of a given situation. That special something that makes our spirits soar and hearts sing.

Zest: Your keenness, passion, and enthusiasm for your life and everything it brings.

The way you react to adversity determines the brightness of the light which shines on the path you travel.

Life continues to unfold regardless of the attitude you carry. With a positive and life-enriching outlook, the future can be a great deal brighter and more powerful. Be grateful for every aspect of your life, and realize that even obstacles are blessings because they too hold opportunities if you take the time to look.

Be respectful of your life and appreciate the positive effect you have on others. You have the capacity to be a great role model for so many other people, irrespective of who you are and who they are. It's a powerful weapon for greatness.

Every day, each person you meet can learn something positive from your optimistic attitude. You too can learn so much from people you encounter—in the workplace, on the street, at the gym, on the bus or train, in a café, or even in the classroom.

Negative behavior from others is also a learning tool for you. You can learn powerful lessons in success creation even from pessimistic and harmful treatment at the hands of other individuals. It's important to look at your life with a very positive eye. Realize that every day will not be filled with sunshine, but every encounter, though it might not seem positive on the surface, has the capacity to add depth to your existence. Embrace the power you have to adopt a great attitude in spite of what comes into your life.

If you continue to wait for the right time, you will sit and watch as opportunities continue to pass by your door.

Be proud of who you are and the journey you're undertaking. Though each day is a new dawning, it's important to have a positive and powerful attitude. Never shy away from challenge and embrace obstacles as they arise. They don't necessarily spell the end of something old but the beginning of something brand new.

When you're doing the best you can with the skills you have, you're being true to yourself. Acting with integrity empowers others to do their best in their lives. As a person with integrity, you become a great role model. You develop the skills to enrich and empower others, and in that special role you become a true spiritual leader.

It's now that others begin to view you in a new way, and as you shine your light for the world to follow they are more confident as they choose to emulate your behavior.

Continue your amazing journey. Keep the horizon in view, and if you happen to stray from the path, remain focused and positive as you bring yourself back on track. Embrace challenge and realize your own amazing potential.

Your positive, life-affirming action, attitude, drive, and commitment invariably encourage others to step out of their comfort zones and enjoy all that life has to offer. It's in this great place you have now become an extraordinary force for good in the global community. That's awesome—congratulations!

When you speak from the heart, you rarely speak anything but the truth.
Give others reasons to believe in you.

LESSONS LEARNED

1. There is nothing you can't do, irrespective of who you are or the choices you make. No task is too difficult or challenge too big once you make up your mind to be successful. A positive and powerful state of mind requires action, persistence, and enthusiasm.

2. Embrace life with all its ups and downs, the challenges and obvious blessings. Realize your full potential by understanding your purpose and embracing all that life brings to your door.

3. Respect yourself and others. Be true to yourself and embrace all you are capable of achieving. When you do the best you can with the skills and experience you have, the future begins to unfold for you.

4. Embrace the opportunity to become a role model and mentor for others. Become a true shining light in the world. Never surrender your goals and never, *ever* let go of your dreams.

Imagine the possibilities...

EPILOGUE

*Perfection comes in so many sizes, shapes, and colors.
After all, there are countless people on this earth. We're all
different and we're all perfect if we choose to live our lives
according to a set of positive, life-enriching values.*

Irrespective of who we are or what has impacted our lives, there are times when we can struggle to find our voice. It certainly was my problem for many years. It kept me imprisoned in a cell of solitude and loneliness for what felt like a lifetime. I didn't realize I had an inner strength and power.

It's imperative to have an open mind and heart with every interaction we have. It serves to keep us focused and aware of our surroundings. When our mind and heart are open, we invite positive energy to take up residence in our psyche. It enables us to eliminate negative thoughts from our everyday lives.

When we allow negativity, uncertainty, and a lack of enthusiasm to over-shadow our future, we automatically allow a degree of darkness into our space. It increases our tendency to shy away from challenge. It means that positive action is put on the shelf and procrastination finds a safe haven. We continue to look upon obstacles as issues to be avoided.

While no one likes to face problems, they do add depth and value to our lives when we can examine them objectively and see the opportunity carefully wrapped in the particular issue. As we uncover plausible solutions, we automatically build our resolve and confidence.

> Don't be an armchair sage. Get off the couch and into the ebb and flow of life. Allow others to see you as a mentor rather than an anchor.

It's important to harness our internal power if we are to ever embrace the future and improve our lives. When we feel inspired to do the best we can, the future becomes a more positive place to be.

Through my interaction with countless people on a global scale, I'm convinced we each have a genius residing within us in some aspect of our lives. We each have a gift, waiting to be shared. When we can step out from under the clouds, we embrace the sunshine and allow ourselves to become empowered and enriched.

Realize that change is inevitable. As you change, you evolve. When you embrace success, know that it can deliver you some amazing opportunities. Be positive as often as possible. Know that change brings about a brand new perspective. Appreciate and respect yourself at all times, and value the positive input of those with your best interests at heart.

Embrace your life and all it offers. Find the courage to take up the opportunity to add value to the lives of other people. The future becomes much brighter for all when you encourage others to embrace the future and be the very best they can.

Form positive, life-enriching habits. Know they have extraordinary value in your life. When you can change any negativity for positive behavior, it adds far greater depth to your life.

> If you want a smooth ride through life, don't have a dream, a vision, or a plan. You'll never embrace success if you don't encounter obstacles. They're part and parcel of the journey, because inside every one lies an amazing treasure.

Take up the journey today. Be and do the best you can. Don't shy away from challenge. Face it head on and search for plausible solutions. Be positive and focused as often as you can. Make it a habit in your life. Always maintain your honesty and integrity. Smile often; share a kind word; have time for friends, neighbors, and even complete strangers. Share your joy freely with others; be happy and embrace every possible opportunity to be a mentor in the lives of other people.

I appreciate your support and invite you to come by the website (kieran-revell.com). Share in the discussions and let others learn from your individual journey. You are an amazing person with a great deal to offer. Share the highs and lows and learn from the experience of fellow travelers. Make your life a shining light for other people to emulate.

Capitalize on all the resources you'll find and let me know how well you're doing. Every day won't be a bed of roses, but you will find blossoms among the thorns. Embrace your self-worth and never underestimate your own true value. Let that internal light shine for the benefit of all.

Join the blogs and forums and freely share your ideas and passions with other like-minded people. Your story might just be the catalyst necessary to assist someone else to step from the shadows and shine.

Once you realize your own dream and have a clear and unimpeded vision of your future, you have a much clearer view of the world around you. Others too will see and appreciate the new you as your confidence grows and you exude a very positive persona.

Read my many e-zine posts and drop by my YouTube channel for some motivational tips and ideas. They're designed to assist you on your magnificent journey. All the material is intended to support and encourage your voyage into the future.

With passion and determination you can achieve anything you put your mind to. As you embrace and celebrate your own true magnificence, the future takes on a whole new meaning. The possibilities for amazing success become limitless.

You must believe without reservation that you are a truly wonderful person capable of great things. Learn lessons and continue to grow. Make yourself accessible and share your time freely with others.

As you evolve, you become a shining example. You soon find yourself surrounded by a community of like-minded people who are also passionate, focused, driven, and optimistic. It's time to embrace the spiritual leader within.

Imagine the possibilities...

Don't waste your time striving for greatness. It already resides deep within. We need only speak the truth with compassion and generosity. The greatness will find its way into the hearts and minds of others.

ABOUT KIERAN REVELL

When you are not pretending to be anyone but yourself, you extend
a helping hand to others striving to find their way in the world.

From his childhood and through his teenage years, Kieran Revell suffered
under the weight of an almost unbearable speech stammer. There were long
periods of darkness and misery. He was bullied and made to feel inadequate.
Those years were a constant spiral into a vast well of solitude.

Eventually Kieran found hope as he mustered the courage and determination to conquer his affliction. For the first time in ten years he was able to
walk out into the sunlight of opportunity and enjoy his new-found freedom.

Kieran also had a near drowning episode at age 17, when he believed he
received a message from his long-dead grandparents. As life ebbed from him,
they came with a message of hope. They told him, "You have an Unstoppable
Power Within." "You have a message of hope for the world." "The time will
come when you can Release Your Power Within for the benefit of humanity."

That message of hope has remained with him all his life, and as he has
grown he has also evolved with he memories of his many life experiences and
the words of his grandparents resonating loudly in his heart and his mind.

With the memory of what he had been told so long ago, Kieran some years
ago realized it was time to embrace his purpose. He took the extraordinary

step of moving out of his comfort zone for a week to live on the streets. He saw it as an ideal way to understand the plight of the homeless.

> Every great dish requires some superb ingredients. What's your recipe for a successful life?

During that challenging period, Kieran met many wonderful characters. He was saddened by the extraordinary stories of loss, illness and injury, business failures, family breakdowns, and tragedies. It proved to be a time of real spiritual growth and development in spite of the fact that he was abused, jostled, and insulted not by the homeless people, but by passers-by. He was called a *bum*, a *freeloader*, a *lowlife*, a *maggot*, and many other more colorful names. For the first time in his life, he understood the pain and anguish silently suffered by those members of society who continue to fall through the cracks.

It was a time of extraordinary growth where he refused to lose his resolve. As each moment passed and through each encounter he had, Kieran continued on his amazing journey of personal awakening. This experience forms the basis of an upcoming book.

Kieran has gone on to become an International Executive Leadership Consultant and speaker, coach, mentor, and author. He specializes in all aspects of Spiritual Leadership.

He has made it his mission to assist others—corporate leaders, business owners, and individuals—to add depth, color, and diversity to their lives. It has become an extraordinary journey of personal and professional realization.

> Happiness is freedom. It has no boundaries or conditions. Embrace it fully and watch as your present brightens and the future expands.

Kieran has studied the many aspects of personal development for more than 25 years. Inspiration, determination, focus, and gratitude remain constants in his approach to fulfillment.

His knowledge, passion, and advanced programs deliver the tools, resources, and strategies necessary for individuals and corporations to step out of the shadows and grow.

He assists clients to improve workplace harmony, nurture and encourage team spirit, strengthen personal and professional relationships, reignite self-confidence and respect, develop effective communication skills, streamline goals, and maximize human potential and peak performance in the realization of unimaginable dreams.

A sought-after keynote speaker, Kieran believes totally in the power of the Self, and through his warm and endearing nature he empowers individuals, groups, and corporations to understand and appreciate the inherent ability to achieve extraordinary growth.

Kieran's functional programs clear pathways to greater success and empowerment. They enable clients to discover a wider appreciation of life through initiating improvement strategies for the instigation of a functional work/life balance and stronger and longer lasting personal and professional relationships.

Kieran teaches effective culture change initiatives in unique and upbeat corporate, group, and individual seminars and training programs. A fresh and driven thought leader, he uncovers the gifts of compassion, inspiration, generosity, determination, focus, communication, and action in clients enabling them to join the dots connecting dreams to reality. He assists them to embrace the skills and knowledge necessary to transform lives.

> Success fills my life because self-belief is a fundamental component of my existence.

Kieran's strategies constantly challenge individuals and corporations to clear obstacles in their processes to expedite the realization of brilliant performance. This enables the achievement of even greater levels of engagement, retention, and productivity, leading to a remarkable bottom line.

Effective communication is a vitally important component for growth and development in both your personal and professional spheres. Kieran is a specialist who inspires comprehensive and dynamic interaction. His disarming nature and passion for life helps to break down barriers, unlock the power within, and rebuild strong and functional channels. Unleash your power today.

Kieran has always been fascinated by the science of success and all it embodies. Why do some people succeed where others do not, and why does a percentage of the population appear to corner the market on wealth and abundance when others struggle their whole lives with little to show for their effort? These and many other questions continue to fire his passion and imagination. His strategies and programs help to deliver the answers.

> Every success you have in your life is a reward for hard work. Every obstacle is a guidepost designed to bring you back on track to something more rich and powerful.

This book outlines the systematic action Kieran believes is necessary to build an exceptional existence and achieve an extraordinary quality of life, as he has done.

Kieran is available for your next seminar, event, or coaching session, when you make up your mind to put yourself, your family, and your business/company/group on the pathway to indescribable success and prosperity.

Go to www.kieranrevell.com and discover a brand new life. You will find a host of wonderful empowerment tools to assist in getting your life to the next sensational level of existence. Take positive action today to transform your dreams into reality.

Turn the key of opportunity in your life and unlock your magnificent future. Have faith in all you know you are capable of becoming. Unleash your spiritual leader within; empower and enrich those around you so they too might have the opportunity to thrive.

The time for procrastination is over because tomorrow waits for no one. The greatest obstacle to success is your own failure to believe.

Imagine the possibilities...

Positive thinking won't always stop things going wrong. However, when they do, don't lose your resolve. Understand that in that moment, the problems arose for a reason. Get back into the game and continue forward with passion and determination.

SOUND WISDOM BOOKS BY KIERAN REVELL

The Unstoppable Power Within